Favorite Recipes from Pepperidge Farm

DORISON HOUSE PUBLISHERS, INC.
NEW YORK   BOSTON

Foreword

Why another cookbook? Because Pepperidge Farm wants to share with you some old and cherished recipes of times past. Recipes that were favorites in those golden days when time moved more slowly and life was more leisurely.

Home economists at Pepperidge Farm have carefully culled the best from their files, adapted them to today's shorter and quicker methods, tested and re-tested them to be sure that the results were as good as the originals, and now proudly present the collection to you.

We hope *Favorite Recipes From Pepperidge Farm* will increase for you the fun and excitement of creative cooking and add to the pleasure and satisfaction of giving to friends and family food that delights the palate while nourishing the body.

Happy cooking!
Mary McGrath
PEPPERIDGE FARM, INC.

The following products wherever used are
registered trademarks of Pepperidge Farm:
Goldfish Crackers, Goldfish Thins, Pan-Style
Stuffing, and Golden Twist Rolls. Distinctive
cookies: Bordeaux, Brussels, Capri, Lido,
Milano, Nassau, Orleans, and Tahiti.

Copyright ©1979 by Pepperidge Farm, Incorporated
Published by Dorison House Publishers, Inc.
183 Madison Avenue, New York, New York 10016

Photography: Cor Videler
Illustrations: Tom Garcia

ISBN: 916752-34-8

Library of Congress Catalog Number: 79-65555

Manufactured in the United States of America

Contents

Appetizers 5

Soups & Stews 18

Meats 33

Poultry 46

Sea Food 63

Eggs & Cheese 81

Vegetables 92

Salads 105

Sandwiches 117

Desserts 133

Cooking Without Recipes 146

Index 157

Appetizers

Beef Stuffed Mushrooms

16 large mushrooms
3/4 pound ground beef
1/4 cup minced onion
3 tablespoons chopped parsley
1/2 teaspoon salt
1/2 cup Cheese & Garlic Croutons, crushed

Wash mushrooms; remove and chop stems. In a skillet, brown beef with chopped mushroom stems and onion. Stir in parsley and salt. Add all but 2 tablespoons of the crushed croutons. Stuff into mushrooms. Place side by side in a shallow, buttered baking dish. Sprinkle mushrooms with remaining crushed croutons. Bake at 400°F for 8 to 10 minutes, or until mushrooms are tender.

MAKES 8 SERVINGS.

Mini Pizzas

6 English Muffins
1 package (12 ounces) frozen brown-and-serve
    sausages
1-1/2 cups prepared pizza sauce
1 package (8 ounces) Mozzarella cheese, sliced
1/2 cup grated Parmesan cheese

Split English Muffins and cut each half into 2 pieces. Toast cut surfaces. Cook sausages and cut into slices. Place slices on English Muffin pieces. Spoon sauce over sausage slices. Top with Mozzarella cheese slices and grated Parmesan cheese. Place under broiler and broil until cheese is melted and bubbly.

MAKES 24 MINI PIZZAS.

Variations
Omit sausages and use any 1 of the following:

 Sliced frankfurters
 Chopped ham, or leftover cooked meat loaf, or chicken
 Sliced olives or mushrooms
 Anchovy fillets
 Sautéed onions and green peppers

For a luncheon serving, just split muffins and prepare as above.

Chicken-on-the-Rye

1/4 cup chopped almonds
1/2 cup finely chopped and peeled cucumber
1 can (4-3/4 ounces) chicken spread
Mayonnaise
16 to 20 slices Party Rye Bread
Sliced stuffed olives

Toast chopped almonds. Mix with chopped cucumber and chicken spread. Stir in enough mayonnaise to make spreading consistency. Spread generously on Party Rye Bread slices. Garnish with stuffed olive slices. MAKES 16 TO 20 SNACKS.

Blue Cheese Mushroom Dip

1 package (8 ounces) cream cheese at room temperature
1/3 cup sour cream
1 package (4 ounces) blue cheese, crumbled
1/3 cup chopped canned mushrooms
1/4 cup chopped green pepper
1/4 cup chopped green onion
Goldfish Thins

In a bowl, mix all ingredients together except Goldfish Thins. Chill. Serve in a bowl surrounded with any flavor Goldfish Thins. MAKES 1-1/2 CUPS.

Almond Chicken Snacks

1 can (4-3/4 ounces) boned white chicken meat
1/2 cup minced peeled cucumber
1/4 cup finely chopped almonds, toasted
2 tablespoons minced green onion
2 tablespoons mayonnaise
16 slices Party Rye Bread
Sliced stuffed olives (optional)

In a bowl, combine all ingredients except bread; mix well. Spread on bread slices. If desired, garnish with sliced olives. MAKES 8 SERVINGS.

Chicken Liver Appetizer

1/2 pound chicken livers
1/3 cup finely chopped onion
Chicken broth
2 hard-cooked eggs, chopped
2 tablespoons mayonnaise
1 teaspoon Worcestershire sauce
Salt to taste
Goldfish Thins
Party Rye Bread

In a small saucepan, combine livers, onion, and enough chicken broth to cover the livers. Cover and simmer for 10 to 15 minutes, or until livers are tender. Cool in broth and then drain. Chop livers coarsely with onions and place into a bowl. Stir in remaining ingredients, adding salt to taste. Chill. Serve spread on any flavor Goldfish Thins, Party Rye or Pumpernickel Bread, or any bread cut into fingers and toasted.
MAKES 1-1/3 CUPS.

Note: Can also be served spooned on lettuce leaves with tomato wedges as an appetizer salad along with crackers, bread, or toast. Also delicious as a filling for bite-size sandwiches.

Salmon Ball

1 package (8 ounces) cream cheese, softened
1/2 cup flaked salmon
1/2 cup chopped green onion
2 tablespoons sour cream
1 tablespoon lemon juice
1/4 teaspoon dried dill weed
1/8 teaspoon coarsely ground pepper
1/2 cup chopped parsley
Lightly Salted Goldfish Thins

In a bowl, combine all ingredients except parsley and Goldfish Thins. Blend well and shape into a ball. Wrap in plastic wrap and refrigerate at least 1 hour.

Just before serving, roll in parsley and surround on serving platter with Goldfish Thins.
MAKES 1-1/2 CUPS SPREAD.

Pickled Chinese Cucumbers

1 cauliflower, broken into small flowerettes
2 cucumbers, unpeeled and diced
1/2 head green cabbage, cored and diced
6 green peppers, seeded and diced
1 carrot, shredded
2 cups white vinegar
1/4 teaspoon tabasco sauce
1/2 cup sugar
1 teaspoon salt
Parker House Rolls

Cover cauliflowerettes with water and simmer 5 minutes. Drain and add remaining ingredients, except rolls. Simmer uncovered for 20 minutes, stirring occasionally. Remove from heat and let stand at room temperature for 5 hours. Pack into jars and store in refrigerator until needed. Serve on lettuce leaves with buttered Parker House Rolls.

MAKES ABOUT 10 TO 12 SERVINGS.

Cheese Twists

1 package (17-1/4 ounces) frozen Bake It Fresh Puff
   Pastry
1/2 cup grated Parmesan cheese
1 teaspoon paprika
1/4 teaspoon cayenne
1/4 teaspoon salt

Thaw puff pastry 20 minutes, then unfold. Brush each square with water.

Combine remaining ingredients. Sprinkle 1 sheet with the cheese mixture, leaving a 1/8 inch margin around the outside edges. Place second sheet, water side down on top of cheese. Press together lightly with rolling pin. Cut square in half and then cut each half into crosswise strips 1/2 inch wide. Grasping strips at each end, twist in opposite directions about 3 times to form a spiral. Place 1 inch apart on an ungreased baking sheet, pressing the ends down to prevent them from unwinding. Chill 10 minutes. Bake in a preheated hot oven (400°) for about 10 minutes or until well browned. Serve warm.

MAKES 40 TWISTS.

Petite Pâté

1 package (17-1/4 ounces) frozen Bake It Fresh Puff
    Pastry
4 chicken livers
1-1/2 tablespoons instant minced onion
4 tablespoons butter or margarine
2 eggs, hard cooked
Salt and pepper
1 egg, beaten slightly
Paprika
Cayenne pepper

Thaw puff pastry 20 minutes, then unfold. Sauté livers and onion in butter until just cooked, about 5 minutes. (Or flash in microwave oven.) Whirl hard-cooked eggs in blender until chopped coarsely. Add liver mixture, blend to a purée and season to taste with salt and pepper.

On a lightly floured board, roll out each puff pastry sheet to an 11 x 14 inch oblong. Cut each sheet into 4 strips measuring 3-1/2 x 11 inches. Brush each oblong of pastry with beaten egg. Spread each piece of pastry thinly with liver mixture. Roll lengthwise as for jelly roll and brush with beaten egg. Cut each of the 8 rolls into 10 pieces. Place about 1 inch apart on an ungreased baking sheet and if desired, sprinkle with paprika and cayenne pepper. Bake in a preheated hot oven (400°) until puffed and golden, approximately 8 minutes.
MAKES 80 PÂTÉS.

Cucumber Spread

2 cups (1 pound) creamed cottage cheese
1 package (3 ounces) cream cheese, softened
1 package (0.56 ounce) green onion dip mix
1/2 cup minced and peeled cucumber
1/2 cup chopped watercress
1/2 teaspoon dill weed
1 package (6-1/4 ounces) Goldfish Thins
Chopped radishes

In a bowl, mix all ingredients except crackers and radishes. Chill for at least 1 hour. Garnish with radishes. Serve with Goldfish Thins.
MAKES ABOUT 3 CUPS.

Marinated Shrimp

1-1/2 pounds shrimp, cooked, shelled and deveined
1/2 cup bottled Italian dressing
1/4 cup minced green pepper
2 tablespoons minced green onion
1/4 teaspoon celery seed
1/4 teaspoon dry mustard
French Bread, thinly sliced and toasted

In a bowl, combine shrimp with all the other ingredients, except bread. Toss to blend well. Cover and refrigerate at least 2 hours. Toss several times during this time. To serve, arrange on plate and serve with French Bread.
MAKES 8 SERVINGS.

Jamaica Pâté

1 package (17-1/4 ounces) frozen Bake It Fresh Puff
   Pastry
1 pound ground beef
1/2 cup diced smoked ham
1/4 cup diced green pepper
2 tablespoons capers
2 tablespoons instant minced onion
2 tablespoons wine vinegar
1 teaspoon crumbled oregano
1/4 teaspoon pepper
Salt and cayenne pepper to taste
1 egg, beaten

Thaw puff pastry 20 minutes, then unfold. In a large skillet cook beef and ham until brown and crumble. Drain excess fat. Fold in remaining ingredients except egg; cool.

On a lightly floured board, roll each pastry sheet out to a 10-1/2 x 14-inch oblong. Cut each sheet into 12 —3-1/2 inch squares. Place 1 tablespoon meat mixture in center of each square. Brush edges with egg. Fold in half to make a rectangle; pinch to seal edges with tines of fork. Brush with remaining egg. Bake in a preheated moderate oven (375°) for 10 to 15 minutes or until golden.
MAKES 24 PÂTÉS.

Herb-Seasoned Bacon Roll-Ups

1/4 cup butter or margarine
1/2 cup water
1-1/2 cups Herb Seasoned Stuffing
1 egg, slightly beaten
1/2 pound sliced bacon
2 cups applesauce
1 teaspoon ginger

In a saucepan, melt butter in hot water. Add stuffing along with beaten egg; toss together lightly. Shape mixture into small sausage-size pieces, about 1-1/4 inches long. Partially cook bacon strips until very lightly browned; drain on absorbent paper. Cut each slice in half. Wrap 1 bacon strip around each stuffing piece and secure with a toothpick. Place in shallow baking pan. Bake at 375°F for 20 to 25 minutes. Combine applesauce and ginger in a saucepan. Heat until bubbly. Serve bacon roll-ups warm with applesauce.
MAKES 20 TO 25 ROLL-UPS.

Toasted Mushroom Rolls

1/2 pound finely chopped fresh mushrooms
1/4 cup butter
3 tablespoons flour
3/4 teaspoon salt
1 cup (1/2 pint) light cream
2 teaspoons minced chives
1 teaspoon lemon juice
1 loaf (2 pounds) Large Family White Bread
1/2 cup melted butter or margarine
1/2 cup very finely chopped walnuts

Sauté mushrooms in butter for 5 minutes; stir in flour and salt. Blend in cream; stir over medium heat until thick. Stir in chives and lemon juice; cool. Remove crusts from bread slices and using a rolling pin, roll slices thin. Cover with damp towel to keep pliable. Spread each slice with mushroom mixture and roll up. Dip each roll first in melted butter then in chopped nuts. To bake, cut each roll in thirds and place seam side down on an ungreased baking sheet. Bake at 400°F for 10 minutes, or until toasted.
MAKES 102 ROLLS.

Herb-Seasoned Bacon Roll-Ups (p. 12), Marinated Shrimp (p. 11), Crab Deviled Eggs (p. 17), and Cucumber Spread (p. 10)

Liverwurst Pâté

1 pound liverwurst
1/3 cup sliced green onion
3 tablespoons prepared mustard
1 tablespoon horseradish
Chopped parsley
Goldfish Thins or Party Rye Bread Slices

Blend first 4 ingredients together; shape into a ball. Roll in parsley. Chill 1 hour. Serve with any flavor Goldfish Thins or Party Rye Bread Slices.
MAKES 1-1/2 CUPS.

Pumpernibbles

1/2 pound liverwurst
3 tablespoons crumbled blue cheese
2 tablespoons instant minced onion
2 tablespoons sour cream
16 slices Party Pumpernickel Bread
Pimiento strips (optional)

In a bowl, combine all ingredients, except bread; mix well. Spread on bread slices. If desired, garnish with pimiento strips.
MAKES 8 SERVINGS.

Mini Franks

6 frankfurters
1-1/2 cups well-drained sauerkraut
6 slices bacon
1 tablespoon instant minced onion
Parker House or Party Pan Rolls

Cut frankfurters in half, then slash each piece lengthwise, cutting not quite all the way through. Fill slash with sauerkraut. Cut bacon slices in half and wrap each frankfurter with a half slice of bacon. Fasten with toothpicks. Broil, turning occasionally, until bacon is crisp. Sprinkle franks with onion, then remove toothpicks. Separate rolls and split each in half cutting not quite all the way through. Place half a frankfurter into each roll. Heat rolls slightly in a 300°F oven.
MAKES 12 PIECES.

Curried Tuna Spread

2 cans (7 ounces each) tuna, drained and flaked
2 hard-cooked eggs, chopped
1/2 cup chopped stuffed olives
1/2 cup sour cream
1/4 cup minced onion
1 teaspoon curry powder
1 teaspoon lemon juice
Salt to taste
Party Rye Bread

In a bowl, combine all ingredients except bread. Cover and chill. Spread mixture on buttered slices of Party Rye Bread.
MAKES ABOUT 3 CUPS.

Pizza Pastries

1 package (17-1/4 ounces) frozen Bake It Fresh Puff
    Pastry
1 cup chopped fresh mushrooms
2 teaspoons olive oil or butter
1 can (8 ounces) tomato sauce
1 tablespoon instant minced onion
1/4 cup grated Parmesan cheese
1 teaspoon oregano
Salt, pepper and cayenne pepper to taste
1 egg, slightly beaten
Additional grated Parmesan cheese

Thaw puff pastry 20 minutes, then unfold. Sauté mushrooms in olive oil or butter until softened. Stir in tomato sauce, onion, cheese and oregano. Season to taste.

On a lightly floured board, roll out each pastry sheet to a 12-inch square. Brush one of the sheets with egg and place 36 teaspoons of the mixture on egg-brushed sheet, allowing approximately an inch between each spoonful of filling. Cover with remaning sheet. Press dough around mounds of filling. Brush with egg and cut into squares between filling. Sprinkle with additional Parmesan, if desired. Seal squares again by pressing around open sides with flour-dipped fork tines. Place squares approximately 1 inch apart on ungreased baking sheet. Bake in preheated hot oven (400°) for 8 minutes or until puffed and golden.
MAKES APPROXIMATELY 1-1/2 CUPS FILLING; 36 HORS D'OEUVRES.

Corned Beef Spread

1 package (8 ounces) cream cheese, softened
1 cup diced cooked corned beef
1/4 cup diced cucumber pickles
1/4 cup minced green pepper
2 tablespoons minced onion
1 tablespoon horseradish
1/4 tablespoon caraway seeds
1/2 cup sour cream
Party Rye or Pumpernickel Bread slices

In a bowl, combine all ingredients except bread slices and blend well. Cover and chill until ready to serve. Serve on Party Rye or Pumpernickel Bread slices.

MAKES ABOUT 2-1/4 CUPS.

Swedish Sandwiches

1 can (4-3/4 ounces) chunky chicken spread
1 tablespoon prepared Dijon mustard
2 hard-cooked eggs, finely chopped
1/2 teaspoon dried dill weed
1/8 teaspoon ground black pepper
36 slices Party Rye Bread
2 tablespoons butter or margarine
2 tablespoons vegetable oil

In a bowl, mix together chunky chicken spread, mustard, chopped egg, dill, and pepper. Spread mixture on 18 slices Party Rye Bread. Top with remaining slices of bread and lightly press them together.

In a skillet, over moderate heat, melt the butter and add oil. Add the sandwiches, 2 or 3 at a time and grill 2 minutes on each side, or until they are crisp and golden brown. Add more butter and oil if needed. Serve hot.

MAKES 18 APPETIZERS.

Eggplant Dip

1 medium eggplant, cubed
1 cup chopped green pepper
1 cup chopped tomato
3/4 cup chopped red onion
1 large clove garlic, minced
3 tablespoons olive oil
1 cup chili sauce
1/2 teaspoon crushed basil
1/3 cup water
1 package (8 ounces) Small Sandwich Pockets
Butter or margarine, melted

In a large skillet, sauté vegetables and garlic in oil until tender. Stir in chili sauce, basil, and water. Simmer uncovered for 5 minutes, stirring often. Serve warm or chilled. Split Sandwich Pockets into 2 thin layers. Cut each layer into quarters and brush with melted butter. Toast and use for dippers. MAKES ABOUT 3 CUPS.

Crab Deviled Eggs

6 hard-cooked eggs
1/2 cup flaked, cooked crab
2 tablespoons mayonnaise
1 tablespoon capers
1 tablespoon minced green onion
1 teaspoon lemon juice
1/2 teaspoon dry mustard
1/4 teaspoon paprika
Goldfish Crackers

Cut eggs in half lengthwise. Remove yolks; combine in bowl with crab, mayonnaise, capers, onion, lemon juice, and mustard. Mix well. Spoon into egg whites, piling high. Sprinkle with paprika. Serve along with any flavor Goldfish Crackers. MAKES 6 SERVINGS.

Soups & Stews

Tomato Bouillon

1 can (10-3/4 ounces) condensed tomato soup
1 can (10-1/2 ounces) condensed beef bouillon
1 soup-can water
1/2 cup dry Sherry wine

Corn & Molasses Bread

In a saucepan, combine all ingredients except bread. Heat thoroughly over low heat, stirring occasionally. Serve with toasted fingers of bread. MAKES 4 SERVINGS.

Kielbasi and Kraut Stew

1/2 pound bacon, chopped
1 onion, chopped
2 pounds kielbasi (Polish sausage) cut into 1-1/2-inch
        chunks
4 tomatoes, chopped
2 pounds sauerkraut, undrained
1 package (6 ounces) Onion & Garlic Croutons

In a skillet, fry bacon until crisp. Add onion and cook for 5 minutes. Stir in sausage, tomatoes, and sauerkraut. Pour mixture into 9 x 13 x 2-inch baking pan. Sprinkle top with croutons. Bake at 350°F for 30 to 35 minutes, or until top is richly browned. MAKES 6 SERVINGS.

Stuffing Dumplings

3 cups Herb Seasoned Stuffing
3/4 cup boiling chicken broth
3 eggs
1/4 cup finely chopped parsley

In a bowl, mix stuffing and boiling chicken broth. Beat in eggs one at a time. Fold in parsley. To prepare dumplings, with wet hands shape mixture into 12 balls. Drop balls of stuffing into simmering stew.

Cover tightly and simmer for 15 to 20 minutes or until dumplings are puffed slightly. Serve dumplings with stew. MAKES 10 TO 12 SERVINGS.

Gazpacho

2 cloves garlic, minced
1/2 teaspoon crushed oregano
1/4 teaspoon celery salt
1 teaspoon salt
1/4 cup olive oil
8 large ripe tomatoes, peeled*
1 cup chicken broth
1/2 cup finely chopped cucumber
1 cup chopped green pepper
1/2 cup sliced green onion
1 tablespoon cider vinegar

4 slices White Bread, cut in 1/4-inch cubes
3 tablespoons grated Parmesan cheese
2 tablespoons chopped parsley

In a blender container or food processor bowl, combine 1 clove of the garlic, oregano, celery salt, salt, and 2 tablespoons of the oil. Add several tomatoes and process on high until smooth. Pour into a large bowl. Process remaining tomatoes and combine in bowl. Add chicken broth, vegetables, and cider vinegar. Chill.

Just before serving, heat remaining 2 tablespoons oil and 1 garlic clove in small skillet. Add bread cubes and brown, tossing frequently. Toss in cheese and parsley. Serve soup in large bowls, topped with browned bread cubes.

*To peel tomatoes, dip into boiling water for 1 minute, then strip off skin. Remove core.

MAKES 8 TO 10 SERVINGS.

Chilled Pineapple Soup

1 can (20 ounces) crushed pineapple
2 cups (1 pint) sour cream
1 cup dry white wine
1 cup Cheddar & Romano Croutons

Drain pineapple, reserving liquid. To this liquid add water to make 1 cup. In a large mixing bowl, combine sour cream, wine, and liquid from crushed pineapple; mix thoroughly. Stir in drained pineapple and chill for several hours, or overnight. Serve sprinkled with croutons.

MAKES 6 SERVINGS.

Curried Crab Soup

1 cup sliced mushrooms
1/2 cup sliced celery
1/2 cup chopped onion
1/2 cup green pepper strips
1 medium garlic clove, minced
2 tablespoons butter
2 tablespoons flour
3 cups chicken stock or chicken broth
1/2 teaspoon curry
1 cup flaked crab
1 egg yolk
1 cup (1/2 pint) light cream or milk
2 cups Cheese & Garlic Croutons

In a large saucepan, cook mushrooms, celery, onion, green peppers, and garlic in butter until tender. Stir in flour and cook over low heat, stirring until bubbling and smooth. Remove from heat. Gradually stir in chicken broth and curry. Return to heat and cook, stirring constantly, until thickened. Fold in crab. In a small bowl, beat egg yolk with cream. Add some hot soup to egg mixture. Stir this mixture into remaining hot soup. Cook, stirring, until heated and thickened (do not boil). Garnish each serving with croutons.
MAKES 6 SERVINGS.

Cold Yogurt Soup

1/4 cup raisins
2 cups cold water
3 cups plain yogurt
1/4 cup skim milk
1 hard-cooked egg, chopped
1/4 cup finely diced and peeled cucumber
2 tablespoons finely chopped green onion
1/2 teaspoon dill weed
1-1/2 cup Onion & Garlic Croutons

Soak raisins in cold water until puffed. Put yogurt in mixing bowl with skim milk, egg, cucumber, and onion. Stir well. Add raisins and water in which they were soaked. Refrigerate. Serve sprinkled with dill weed and topped with croutons.
MAKES 6 SERVINGS.

Oyster Stew

2 tablespoons flour
1-1/2 teaspoons salt
2 tablespoons water
2 cups shucked raw oysters with liquid
2 cups milk
2 cups (1 pint) heavy cream
Butter pats
Parsley or paprika
Lightly Salted Goldfish Crackers

In a large saucepan, make a paste of the flour, salt, and water. Stir in the oyster liquid until smooth; stir in oysters. Cook over low heat, stirring constantly, until the edges of oysters begin to curl. In another saucepan, combine milk and cream and bring to scalding point. Gradually stir hot milk into oyster mixture; cover and let stand 5 minutes to develop flavor. To serve, ladle into soup bowls and garnish with pats of butter. Sprinkle with parsley or paprika. Serve with Goldfish Crackers.

If it is necessary to reheat oyster stew, never place it over high heat or bring it to a boil. Stir over low heat until soup is hot.
MAKES 6 SERVINGS.

Peanut Soup

6 slices bacon
2 cups chopped celery
1 cup chopped onion
1/4 cup flour
1 cup creamy peanut butter
3 cups well-seasoned chicken broth
2 cups (1 pint) light cream
2 cups Cheddar & Romano Croutons

In a large saucepan, cook bacon. Remove, drain on absorbent paper, and crumble; set aside. Add celery and onions to pan drippings. Cook until tender. Stir in flour and cook, stirring until bubbling and smooth. Gradually stir in peanut butter and chicken broth. Cook, stirring constantly, until thickened and smooth. Reduce heat and simmer 10 minutes, stirring occasionally. Just before serving, stir in cream. Heat but do not boil. Garnish each serving generously with croutons.
MAKES 8 TO 10 SERVINGS.

Spinach Soup

1 package (10 ounces) frozen chopped spinach
2-1/4 cups chicken broth (canned or made from chicken
        bouillon cubes)
1 small onion, chopped
3 tablespoons butter
3 tablespoons flour
2 cups milk
1/2 cup heavy cream
1/4 teaspoon grated nutmeg
1 cup (1/2 pint) sour cream
1 package (6 ounces) Sesame Garlic Goldfish Crackers

In a large saucepan, combine spinach, chicken broth, and onion. Simmer covered for 10 to 15 minutes, or until spinach is cooked. In another saucepan, melt butter and stir in flour. Gradually mix in the milk and cream. Stir over low heat until mixture bubbles and thickens slightly. Stir in spinach, broth, and nutmeg. Season to taste with salt and pepper. Serve at once, topped with sour cream and Goldfish Crackers.
MAKES 6 SERVINGS.

Hot Cinnamon Soup

2 cups cored, diced, unpeeled apple
1 teaspoon ground cinnamon
Generous dash of ground nutmeg
2 tablespoons butter or margarine
3 cups chicken stock or broth
1 cup orange juice
1/2 cup golden raisins

16 Lightly Salted Snack Sticks
3 tablespoons melted butter
1/4 cup toasted coconut

Sauté apple, cinnamon, and nutmeg in butter for several minutes, stirring often. Add chicken broth, orange juice, and raisins. Cover and simmer for 10 minutes.

Meanwhile, toss Snack Sticks in melted butter and then in coconut. Place on ungreased baking sheet. Bake at 350°F for 5 to 7 minutes or until golden. Serve with soup.
MAKES 4 SERVINGS.

Zucchini Soup

4 slices bacon
1 cup sliced onions
4 cups chicken broth
1 can (16 ounces) tomatoes, chopped and drained
2 medium zucchini, sliced
1 pound (about 1 cup) shelled fresh peas
1 teaspoon chopped fresh dill

1/4 cup butter, softened
1 small garlic clove, minced
1 loaf (1 pound) French Bread, thickly sliced and toasted

In a large saucepan, fry bacon. Remove, drain on absorbent paper; crumble. Set aside. Pour off all but 2 tablespoons of the drippings. Cook onions in drippings until tender. Stir in broth, tomatoes, zucchini, peas, and dill. Cover and simmer 20 minutes or until vegetables are tender.

Mix butter and garlic and fold in crumbled bacon. Spread on sliced bread and broil until golden. Serve with soup.
Makes 4 to 6 servings.

Irish Stew

3 pounds boneless lamb, cut into 1-inch cubes
1/3 cup chopped parsley
2 pounds potatoes, peeled and cut into 1-inch cubes
3 large onions, sliced
1/2 teaspoon thyme
Salt and pepper to taste
Water, about 6 cups
1 bag (1 pound, 4 ounces) frozen baby whole onions
8 slices Oatmeal Bread, crusts trimmed and
    crumbled finely

In a Dutch oven or large saucepan, combine lamb, parsley, potatoes, onions, thyme, salt, pepper, and enough water to cover. Cover tightly; simmer for 1 to 1-1/2 hours or until lamb is tender. Add onions and bread crumbs. Cover and simmer, stirring occasionally for 10 to 15 minutes, or until onions are tender and stew is thickened. Season to taste with salt and pepper.
Makes 6 servings.

Three-Meat Stew With Dumplings

2 tablespoons butter or margarine
1 large onion, chopped
3 pounds assorted boneless 1-inch cubes of meat: beef,
    lamb, and veal
Salt and pepper to taste
1 cup pitted black olives
2 cups sliced celery
6 carrots, cut into 1-inch chunks
1 cup rosé wine
Chicken broth, about 2 cups
Stuffing Dumplings (see page 19)

In a Dutch oven or large saucepan, heat butter and sauté onion for 5 minutes. Add meat, which has been seasoned with salt and pepper, and brown meat cubes on all sides. Add olives, celery, carrots, wine, and enough chicken broth to cover meat and vegetables. Cover tightly and simmer gently for 1 to 1-1/2 hours, or until meat is tender. If desired, stew may be thickened with 1/4 cup flour mixed with 1/2 cup water. Prepare stuffing dumplings according to recipe directions. Drop balls into simmering stew. Cover tightly and simmer for 15 to 20 minutes, or until dumplings are puffed slightly.

MAKES 10 TO 12 SERVINGS.

Strawberry Soup

3 pints fresh strawberries
Juice of 1 lemon
2-1/2 cups water
1 cup sugar
2 tablespoons quick-cooking tapioca
1 cup dry white wine
2 cups Cheese & Romano Croutons
1/4 cup chopped fresh mint

Hull and wash strawberries. Purée in blender or processor, or crush with potato masher. In a saucepan, combine fruit and lemon juice. Add water, sugar, and tapioca. Bring to a boil. Reduce heat and simmer for 15 minutes. Stir occasionally; remove from heat. Stir in wine and chill thoroughly. Serve topped with Cheese & Romano Croutons and mint.

MAKES 8 TO 10 SERVINGS.

Three-Meat Stew With Dumplings

Lentil Soup Parmesan

2 stalks celery with leaves
2 carrots, peeled
1 medium leek
1 medium onion
3 tablespoons butter
3 tablespoons flour
6 cups hot water, or beef or chicken broth
1 bay leaf
1/4 teaspoon crushed thyme
2 teaspoons salt
1-1/2 cups lentils, washed and sorted
1/2 cup diced turnip
2 cups Parmesan Cheese Goldfish Crackers

Coarsely chop first 4 vegetables. Sauté vegetables in butter in large saucepan until tender. Stir in flour and cook, stirring until smooth and bubbling. Remove from heat and gradually stir in water or hot broth. Stir in remaining ingredients except crackers. Simmer partially covered for 1 hour, or until lentils and turnips are tender. Purée soup in a food mill, processor, or blender and reheat. Season to taste, if necessary, with additional salt and pepper. Garnish with Goldfish Crackers.
MAKES 8 TO 10 SERVINGS.

Sprouted Wheat Onion Soup

1/4 cup butter or margarine
6 large onions, thinly sliced
6 cups beef broth
1/3 cup Marsala wine
3 tablespoons Worcestershire sauce
6 slices toasted Sprouted Wheat Bread
1 package (8 ounces) Mozzarella cheese, sliced
6 tablespoons grated Parmesan cheese

In a large, heavy saucepan, heat butter. Add onions and sauté until golden. Add beef broth, wine, and Worcestershire sauce. Simmer covered for 20 to 30 minutes, or until onions are tender. Top bread slices with Mozzarella cheese and place under broiler until cheese is melted. Serve onion soup in large bowls and top with bread and cheese slices. Sprinkle with Parmesan cheese.
MAKES 6 SERVINGS.

French Lamb and Eggplant Stew

1/3 cup olive oil
2 cloves garlic, chopped
1 large onion, chopped
1 cup sliced celery
1/2 teaspoon fines herbes
3 pounds boneless lamb, cut into 1-inch cubes
Salt and pepper to taste
3 cups tomato vegetable juice
1 can (1 pound) stewed tomatoes
4 zucchini, diced
1/2 pound mushrooms, trimmed and sliced
1 small eggplant, diced
French Bread or Rolls

In a large saucepan or Dutch oven, heat oil and sauté garlic, onion, and celery for 5 minutes. Add fines herbes, lamb sprinkled with salt and pepper, tomato juice, and tomatoes. Cover and simmer for 1 to 1-1/2 hours or until lamb is tender. Add vegetables and continue cooking covered until vegetables are tender and stew is thickened, about 20 to 25 minutes. Season to taste with salt and pepper. Serve with heated, crusty French Bread or Rolls.

MAKES 6 SERVINGS.

Hungarian Pork and Vegetable Goulash

1/4 cup butter or margarine
3 pounds boneless pork, cut into 1-inch cubes
2 tablespoons paprika
Salt and pepper to taste
2 Idaho potatoes, peeled and finely diced
2 large onions, sliced
Water, about 6 cups
1/2 pound green beans, trimmed and cut into
    1-inch pieces
3 carrots, cut into 1-inch pieces
3 cups coarsely chopped green cabbage
Rye Bread

In a Dutch oven or large saucepan, melt butter and brown pork cubes on all sides. Sprinkle with paprika, salt, and pepper. Add potatoes, onions, and enough water to cover. Cover and simmer for 1 to 1-1/2 hours, or until pork is tender. Add remaining vegetables, cover and simmer for another 15 to 20 minutes, or until vegetables are tender. If desired, stew may be thickened with 1/4 cup flour mixed with 1/3 cup water. Season again with salt and pepper. Serve with toasted slices of Rye Bread which have been rubbed with a clove of garlic and spread thinly with butter. MAKES 6 SERVINGS.

Texas Chili Stew With Cheese Pockets

1 pound ground chuck
1 onion, minced
2 eggs
1/2 cup crushed Herb Seasoned Stuffing
1 teaspoon salt
1 tablespoon oil
1 can (1 pound) stewed tomatoes, undrained
1 can (15 ounces) kidney beans, drained
1 package (1-3/4 ounces) chili seasoning mix
2 cups beef broth

1 package (8 ounces) Small Sandwich Pockets
1/2 pound Mozzarella or Monterey Jack cheese cut into
    thin slices

In a bowl, mix chuck, onion, eggs, stuffing, and salt. Shape mixture with wet hands into 1-inch balls. In a skillet, heat oil and brown meat balls slowly on all sides until cooked. Add tomatoes, beans, seasoning mix, and beef broth. Simmer, stirring occasionally for 20 minutes, or until stew is thickened.

Cut Sandwich Pockets in half and open slightly. Fill pockets with cheese slices. Place on cookie sheet in a 350°F oven for 10 to 15 minutes or until cheese is melted. Serve stew in bowls with cheese pockets. MAKES 4 SERVINGS.

Cold Cherry Soup

1 pound fresh sour cherries, pitted; or 2 cups canned
    sour cherries, drained
1 can (8-1/4 ounces) crushed pineapple, undrained
1 cup orange juice
2 tablespoons sugar

1 package (8 ounces) cream cheese, softened
1/4 cup chopped toasted pecans
1/4 cup chopped golden raisins
1 package (7 ounces) Old-Fashioned Rolls, split

Place cherries in blender container. Blend on high until smooth. Pour into bowl. Add pineapple, orange juice, and sugar. Chill. Just before serving, mix cream cheese, pecans, and raisins. Spread on rolls. Serve with soup.
MAKES 6 SERVINGS.

Fresh Pea Soup

1 cup sliced green onions
2 tablespoons butter or margarine
2 tablespoons flour
1 quart beef broth
3 cups cubed peeled potatoes
3 cups fresh shelled peas
1/2 cup sour cream
1 tablespoon chopped fresh dill
1/2 teaspoon salt
Snack Sticks

In a large, heavy saucepan, cook onions in butter until tender. Stir in flour. Gradually stir in beef broth. Cook over low heat, stirring constantly, until thickened and smooth. Stir in potatoes, peas, sour cream, dill, and salt. Cover and simmer for 20 minutes, or until vegetables are tender. Season to taste with additional salt. Serve with any flavor Snack Sticks.
MAKES 6 SERVINGS.

West Coast Fish Stew

1/3 cup olive oil
1 onion, chopped
1 cup chopped celery and leaves
1 clove garlic, chopped
1 small green pepper, seeded and chopped
1 can (1 pound, 12 ounces) tomatoes, undrained
1 can (8 ounces) tomato sauce
1 cup dry red wine
1 teaspoon sugar
1 teaspoon salt
1/4 teaspoon each basil and oregano

1 pound cod or haddock, cut into 2-inch pieces
1 pound raw shrimp, shelled and deveined
12 small clams, scrubbed
2 frozen rock lobster tails (4 ounces each), cut
    into 1-inch cross-section pieces
English Muffins or Toasting White Bread

In a large saucepan, heat olive oil and sauté onion, celery, garlic, and green pepper until golden, about 5 minutes. Add tomatoes, tomato sauce, wine, sugar, salt, basil, and oregano. Cover and simmer for 20 minutes. Add fish and shellfish. Cover and simmer for another 15 to 20 minutes, or until clams open. Season, if necessary, with salt and pepper. Serve with split and toasted English Muffins or with slices of toasted Toasting White Bread.

MAKES 6 SERVINGS.

New England Fish Chowder

1 pound flounder, haddock, or cod fillet, cut into
    1-inch pieces
Water
4 slices bacon
1 cup chopped onions
1/2 cup chopped green pepper
1 cup diced cooked potatoes
1/4 cup flour
2 cups milk
1/2 teaspoon crushed thyme
1 teaspoon salt
1/8 teaspoon pepper
1 cup (1/2 pint) light cream

1 package (10 ounces) Brown-and-Serve French Rolls
6 tablespoons softened butter
1/4 cup blue cheese

Place fish in large saucepan or Dutch oven and add enough water to cover. Bring to a boil, cover and simmer for 15 minutes or until fish is tender. Drain fish, reserve stock, and keep fish warm. In a large saucepan, fry bacon, remove, and drain on absorbent paper; crumble. Cook onions, green pepper, and potatoes several minutes in bacon drippings until tender but not brown, stirring frequently. Stir in flour; remove from heat and gradually stir in reserved fish stock, milk, thyme, salt, and pepper. Return to heat and cook, stirring constantly until thickened and smooth. Fold in fish broken into pieces, and cream. Heat but do not boil. Season to taste with additional salt and pepper.

Split rolls. Mix crumbled bacon with butter and blue cheese. Spread on rolls and bake according to package directions until rolls are golden. Serve with soup.

MAKES 6 SERVINGS.

Belgian Beef-and-Beer Stew With Crouton Dumplings

STEW

3 pounds boneless beef chuck, cut into 1-inch cubes
Salt, pepper, flour
1/3 cup vegetable shortening
6 large onions, quartered
2 cloves garlic, chopped
1 can (10-1/2 ounces) condensed beef broth, undiluted
1/2 teaspoon crumbled thyme
2 to 3 cups beer

DUMPLINGS

2 cups biscuit mix
2 eggs
1/3 cup milk
2 teaspoons instant minced onion
1/4 cup finely chopped parsley
1 cup Seasoned Croutons with Herbs and Cheese

Sprinkle beef with salt and pepper; roll in flour. Heat shortening in a Dutch oven and brown beef cubes on all sides. Add onions, garlic, beef broth, thyme, and 2 cups of the beer. Cover tightly and simmer for 1 to 1-1/2 hours, or until beef is tender. If necessary, add remaining beer from time to time to keep up the level of liquid.

In a bowl, combine biscuit mix, eggs, milk, onion, and parsley; mix until well blended. Fold in croutons. Drop mixture by heaping tablespoons into simmering stew. Cover and simmer for 15 to 20 minutes, or until dumplings are firm to the touch. Place dumplings on serving plate and top with stew.

MAKES 6 SERVINGS.

Meats

Ham Divan

2 packages (10 ounces each) frozen broccoli
    spears, thawed
6 large slices cooked ham or luncheon meat
1 can (10-1/2 ounces) condensed golden mushroom soup
1/2 cup milk
1 cup (4 ounces) grated sharp cheese
Dash of pepper
1/2 teaspoon prepared mustard
1 cup Herb Seasoned Stuffing
4 tablespoons melted butter or margarine

In a shallow 1-1/2-quart baking dish, place broccoli with stems pointing toward the center. Arrange ham slices over broccoli stems.

In a saucepan, mix soup, milk, cheese, pepper, and mustard. Heat, stirring, until cheese is melted. Pour over ham in baking dish. Lightly toss stuffing and butter and sprinkle over casserole. Bake at 350°F for 35 minutes, or until topping is golden brown.
MAKES 6 SERVINGS.

Grilled Stuffed Spareribs

6 pounds country-style spareribs (loin backbones)
Salt and pepper to taste
2 tablespoons melted butter
1/2 medium-size onion, chopped
1 package (8 ounces) Herb Seasoned Stuffing
2 tart apples, peeled, cored and chopped
1-1/2 cups drained sauerkraut
1/2 teaspoon marjoram

Sprinkle ribs with salt and pepper. Bake at 350°F for 1 hour. Drain excess fat. Heat butter and sauté onion until wilted, about 5 minutes. In a bowl, mix stuffing, apples, sauerkraut, marjoram, sautéed onions, and pan juices.

Place half of the ribs in a foil-lined deep baking or roasting pan. Spoon stuffing mixture over ribs. Place remaining ribs, meat side up, over stuffing. Bake ribs, covered, at 350°F for about 45 minutes. Remove cover, drain excess fat and bake another 15 to 20 minutes, or until ribs are brown.
MAKES 6 TO 8 SERVINGS.

Hamburger Pie

1 pound ground beef
1/2 cup crumbled Sprouted Wheat Bread
1 cup (4 ounces) shredded Cheddar cheese
1 egg, well beaten
1/4 cup catsup
2 teaspoons instant minced onion
1/2 teaspoon salt
1/8 teaspoon pepper
1/2 teaspoon sweet basil
1 frozen Deep Dish Pie Shell
Shredded Cheddar cheese

In a skillet, brown ground beef until it loses red color; remove from heat. Stir in bread, cheese, egg, catsup, onion, salt, pepper and sweet basil; mix well. Remove pie from freezer. Spoon mixture into frozen pie shell; sprinkle top with cheese. Bake at 350° for 30 minutes.
MAKES 4 TO 6 SERVINGS.

Canned Ham in a Blanket

2 packages (10 ounces each) frozen Bake It Fresh
    Patty Shells
1 small canned ham (2 or 3 pounds)
2 tablespoons prepared mustard
1/2 teaspoon ground cloves
3 to 4 slices canned pineapple
1 egg, beaten

Thaw Patty Shells in package in refrigerator overnight. Open canned ham and rinse juice off under cold water; dry. Spread mustard over top and sides, sprinkle ground cloves over top. Place pineapple on top.

On a lightly floured board, stack 4 of the Patty Shells and roll out until 1-inch larger than the bottom of the ham. Place on shallow baking pan; place ham on pastry. Stack remaining Patty Shells and roll out large enough to cover top and sides of ham. Moisten edges with beaten egg and press firmly to seal. Trim any excess pastry and, if desired, use scraps to decorate top. Brush top and sides with beaten egg, then decorate and brush again. Bake in a preheated hot oven (400°F) for 35 minutes or until the top is golden brown.
MAKES 4 TO 6 SERVINGS.

Hamburger Pie

Lamb and Eggplant Bake

2 pounds lean ground lamb
1 cup Corn Bread Stuffing
1 tablespoon instant onion
2 tablespoons chopped green pepper
1/2 teaspoon salt
1/8 teaspoon pepper
Pinch of ground ginger
1 medium eggplant
1 egg, beaten
1/2 cup Corn Bread Stuffing, crushed
1 tablespoon flour
1/8 teaspoon garlic powder
Vegetable oil
1 can (8 ounces) tomato sauce
2 tablespoons grated Parmesan cheese
2 tablespoons butter or margarine

In a large bowl, mix lamb, stuffing, onion, green pepper, salt, pepper, and ginger. Set aside. Peel eggplant and cut into 6 to 8 slices. Dip each slice into beaten egg, turning to coat both sides. Mix stuffing crumbs, flour, and garlic powder. Press each slice of eggplant into the crumbs, covering both sides. In a large frying pan, heat oil and fry each slice on both sides until browned. Add more oil as necessary. Drain eggplant on absorbent paper. Place half of the eggplant on bottom of a 9-inch baking pan. Top with ground lamb mixture, pressing lamb into an even layer; add remaining eggplant. Spread tomato sauce over the top, sprinkle with cheese and dot with butter. Bake at 350°F for 40 to 45 minutes.
Serves 6 to 8 people.

Beef Wellington

2 packages (10 ounces each) frozen Bake It Fresh
    Patty Shells
1 fillet of beef, about 2-1/2 to 3 pounds
1/4 cup softened butter or margarine
1 can (4 ounces) chopped mushrooms, drained
2 cans (4-3/4 ounces each) liver pâté
1/4 teaspoon rosemary
1 egg
1 teaspoon milk

Thaw Patty Shells in package in refrigerator overnight. Spread top of fillet with softened butter or margarine. Roast in a hot oven (450°F) for 60 minutes (medium rare), then cool completely.

Meanwhile, combine chopped mushrooms, liver pâté, and rosemary. When beef is cool, spread liver-mushroom mixture over entire surface. Stack Patty Shells and press down firmly. Roll out to about 1/4-inch thick making 1 long piece of pastry large enough to enclose beef fillet. Wrap around fillet. Trim edges of pastry, moistening edges with water and seal by pressing together. Brush crust with egg beaten with milk. Prick crust in a few places to allow steam to escape. Roll out trimmed pastry and cut into narrow strips. Lay across dough-wrapped beef in lattice pattern. Brush these also with beaten egg and milk. Bake in preheated hot oven (425°F) for 20 minutes, or until pastry is golden brown.
MAKES 8 TO 10 SERVINGS.

Bavarian Pot Roast

3 pounds beef chuck or blade roast
Garlic salt to taste
Pepper to taste
2 tablespoons oil
1 cup beer
1 can (8 ounces) tomato sauce
1/4 cup cider vinegar
1 tablespoon cinnamon
2 tablespoons sugar
1/2 cup chopped onions
2 bay leaves
6 carrots, cut into 1-inch pieces
6 small white onions, left whole
6 small potatoes, peeled and diced

Sprinkle roast with garlic salt and pepper. Heat oil in a Dutch oven or large saucepan and brown meat on all sides. Mix 1/2 cup of the beer, tomato sauce, vinegar, cinnamon, sugar, and onions in a bowl. Pour over meat. Add bay leaves. Cover tightly and simmer for 1-1/2 to 2 hours, or until meat is tender. Add remaining beer from time to time to keep up the level of the liquid. Skim excess fat from pan juices. Add vegetables, cover and simmer for 15 to 20 minutes, or until vegetables are tender. Cut roast into thick slices and serve with vegetables and pan juices.
MAKES 6 SERVINGS.

Scotch Lamburger Pies

1 package (17-1/4 ounces) frozen Bake It Fresh Puff
    Pastry
2 pounds ground lamb
1/2 cup chopped celery
1 tablespoon instant minced onion
1/4 cup chopped parsley
1/4 teaspoon sage
1/4 teaspoon salt
1/8 teaspoon black pepper
1 cup corn bread stuffing
1/4 cup plain yogurt or sour cream
1 egg, beaten

Thaw puff pastry 20 minutes, then unfold. In a large mixing bowl, thoroughly mix lamb, celery, onion, parsley, sage, salt, black pepper and stuffing. Stir in yogurt or sour cream until mixture is bound together. Shape mixture into 8 generous size meat patties. Cut each pastry sheet into 4 squares. On a lightly floured board, roll out each square about 1-1/2 inches larger than meat patties. Set the patties in center of square and fold pastry over meat, sealing edges in the center. Place seam side down on a baking sheet and brush with beaten egg. Bake in preheated oven (400°) for 20 minutes.
MAKES 8 SERVINGS.

Stuffed Acorn Squash

1/2 pound ground lean beef
1/2 pound ground pork
1 cup Herb Seasoned Stuffing
1 cup consommé
3 acorn squash
Butter or margarine, melted

Mix beef, pork, stuffing, and consommé. Cut acorn squash in half and discard seeds. Parboil the squash by placing cut-side down, in 1 inch of boiling salted water. Cover and simmer about 5 minutes. Remove from water and brush inside generously with melted butter. Fill the squash shells with meat and stuffing mixture and place in a shallow baking pan with 1/2 cup of water. Bake at 350°F for 1 hour, or until squash is tender.
MAKES 6 SERVINGS.

Stuffed Flank Steak

2 cups Onion & Garlic Croutons
1 egg, beaten with 1/2 cup beef broth
1/2 cup chopped onion
1/2 cup chopped celery
1 flank steak (2 to 3 pounds) pounded thin
    (round steak can also be used)
Salt and pepper to taste
3 tablespoons butter or margarine
1 carrot, sliced
1 tomato, sliced
1 onion, sliced
1 teaspoon sweet basil
1/8 teaspoon thyme
1 can (10-1/2 ounces) condensed beef bouillon
1 cup dry red wine
2 tablespoons flour

Mix croutons, egg mixture, onion, and celery. Spread on steak and roll like jelly roll, starting at the short side of the flank steak. Tie roll with string in 3 or 4 places and sprinkle with salt and pepper.

Heat butter or margarine in Dutch oven and brown meat roll on all sides. Add carrot, tomato, onion, basil, thyme, beef bouillon, and wine. Cook covered over low heat for 1-1/2 to 2 hours. Remove meat to platter and thicken sauce with flour mixed with 1/2 cup cold water. To serve, remove string, slice, and spoon sauce over meat.
MAKES 6 SERVINGS.

Juicy Meat Loaf

4 slices Oatmeal, Sprouted Wheat, or Cracked Wheat
    Bread, cut into 1/2-inch cubes
1/2 cup milk
2 pounds ground chuck
1/2 teaspoon black pepper
2 teaspoons salt
2 eggs, beaten
1 large onion, chopped
2 tart apples, peeled, cored and chopped
2 teaspoons fresh lemon juice
1/4 cup Parmesan cheese

In a large bowl, mix bread and milk. Let stand for 10 minutes. Add remaining ingredients except cheese and mix until well blended. Shape meat with hands into a long loaf, about 4 inches wide. Place on a greased baking pan; sprinkle top with cheese. Bake at 350°F for 1 hour.
Makes 6 to 8 servings.

Baked Orange Pork Chops

6 lean pork chops
Salt and pepper to taste
1 large seedless orange
1/2 cup orange juice
1 egg, beaten
2 tablespoons cold water
1-1/2 cups Herb Seasoned Stuffing, crushed

Trim excess fat from chops. Sprinkle chops with salt and pepper. Cut orange into 6 slices and place in bottom of shallow pan. Cover with orange juice. Beat egg and water. Dip each pork chop into egg and roll in stuffing crumbs. Place each chop on top of orange slice, cover with foil, and bake at 350°F for 30 minutes. Remove foil and bake 10 minutes, or until top crumbs of chops are browned.
Makes 6 servings.

Stuffed Chops in Foil

4 thick pork chops
Salt and pepper to taste
5 tablespoons melted butter
1-1/2 cups Herb Seasoned Stuffing
1 large tart apple, unpeeled, cored and chopped
1/4 cup chopped celery
1/4 cup chopped onion

Trim excess fat from pork chops; sprinkle with salt and pepper. Add melted butter to stuffing; toss with apple, celery, and onion. Tear off 2-foot length of heavy duty aluminum foil. In center of foil, stand chops on edge, fat side up. Run 3 long skewers through center of chops, spacing chops about 1 inch apart. Spoon stuffing between chops and around outside. Bring foil over chops and seal securely. If foil becomes punctured, wrap in second layer to assure moisture will stay inside. Bake at 375°F for 1-1/2 hours.
Makes 4 servings.

Lemon Veal and Chinese Cabbage

1 medium Chinese cabbage, sliced
3 tablespoons butter or margarine, melted
1 tablespoon chopped parsley
Salt and pepper to taste
6 to 8 veal scallopini
1/4 cup milk
1 cup Onion & Garlic Croutons, crumbled
1/4 cup vegetable oil
Juice of 1 lemon

Place Chinese cabbage in 1 inch of boiling water. Cover and simmer for 10 minutes. Drain and place on bottom of small casserole. Mix butter and parsley. Pour mixture over cabbage, seasoning to taste with salt and pepper. Place cabbage in a warm oven (about 250°F) until veal is ready.

Soak veal in milk. Using a rolling pin, blender, or food processor, crush croutons until very fine. Press each veal scallopini into crumbs and fry in hot oil in a skillet. Drain on absorbent paper. Spoon cabbage on serving platter and top with veal. Sprinkle lemon juice over top just before serving.
MAKES 6 TO 8 SERVINGS.

Variation
Instead of veal, use skinless and boneless chicken breast halves, pounded until 1/4-inch thick.

Ham Turnovers

1 package (17-1/4 ounces) frozen Bake It Fresh Puff
   Pastry
2 cups chopped cooked lean ham
3 tablespoons light cream or evaporated milk
2 tablespoons chopped onions
1 teaspoon prepared mustard
1/8 teaspoon pepper

Thaw puff pastry 20 minutes, then unfold. Combine ham, cream, onion, mustard and pepper. Mix well and set aside. Cut pastry sheets into 8 — 5 inch squares. Place about 1/4 cup of ham mixture in center of each square. Moisten edges of pastry with water and fold over to form a triangle. Seal edges by pressing down with tine of a fork. Place

turnovers on a baking sheet. Bake in a preheated hot oven (425°) for 12 to 15 minutes or until golden brown. Serve immediately.
MAKES 4 SERVINGS. (8 TURNOVERS)

Veal Oskar

1 package (10 ounces) frozen Bake It Fresh
    Patty Shells
2 tablespoons vegetable oil
1/4 teaspoon garlic powder
6 small pieces veal scallopini
6 slices cooked ham (thin sliced)
1-1/2 cups Herb Seasoned Stuffing
1/2 cup chopped celery
1/4 cup chopped onion
2 tablespoons chopped green pepper
1 package (10 ounces) frozen tiny shelled and
    deveined shrimp, thawed and drained
1 can (10-3/4 ounces) condensed cream of
    shrimp soup
2 tablespoons white wine

Thaw Patty Shells in package in refrigerator overnight. Heat vegetable oil in skillet with garlic powder and cook veal until white in color. Drain on absorbent paper and set aside with ham slices.

In a large bowl, mix stuffing, celery, onion, green pepper, shrimp, shrimp soup, and white wine. Roll out Patty Shell rounds 2 inches larger than the size of the piece of veal. Place veal in center. Press together 2 to 3 tablespoons of stuffing mixture, place on top of veal and cover with a piece of ham. Brush the edges of the pastry with water, and bring up sides sealing at the center of the top. Place seam side down on cookie sheet. Bake in preheated hot (400°F) oven for 15 to 20 minutes, or until shell is golden brown. Serve with your favorite hollandaise sauce.
MAKES 6 SERVINGS.

Easy Pork Roast

4 pork chops
2 tablespoons vegetable shortening
1 cup water
1/2 cup butter or margarine
2 cups Corn Bread Stuffing
1 cup unpeeled, diced apple
1 can (8 ounces) whole cranberry sauce
1/2 cup raisins

Brown chops lightly in hot shortening. Remove from skillet and drain excess fat. Add water and butter to drippings in skillet. Stir in stuffing, apple, cranberry sauce, and raisins. Spread stuffing evenly in a buttered 9-inch square baking pan. Cover the stuffing with browned chops and cover baking pan. Bake at 325°F for 1 hour.
MAKES 6 TO 8 SERVINGS.

Apricot Stuffed Spareribs

SPARERIBS
2 racks spareribs, about 6 pounds
1 package (8 ounces) Herb Seasoned Stuffing
1 can (10 ounces) apricot halves, drained and chopped
1/2 cup chopped celery
1/2 cup sliced almonds
1/2 cup water

BASTING SAUCE
2 cups water
1/4 cup cider vinegar
2 white onions, thinly sliced
1/2 cup raisins
1 lemon, thinly sliced
1/2 cup maple syrup
1 teaspoon allspice
1/2 cup gingersnap crumbs

Lay a rack of spareribs, bone side up, in a foil-lined large roasting pan or jelly-roll pan. In a large bowl, mix stuffing, apricots, celery, almonds, and water. Spread stuffing mixture over the ribs in the roasting pan. Cover with second rack of ribs, meat side up. Bake at 350°F for 1 hour.

Meanwhile, combine basting sauce ingredients in a saucepan. Boil

for about 10 minutes, or until sauce is thick. Drain excess fat from ribs. Lower heat to 325°F and baste the top of the ribs with the sauce. Continue to bake for 30 minutes, occasionally basting the ribs generously with sauce. Heat any leftover sauce and serve with spareribs.
MAKES 4 TO 6 SERVINGS.

Mock Crown Roast of Lamb

LAMB
6 to 8 lamb chops
Salt and pepper to taste
2 cups Herb Seasoned Stuffing
2 teaspoons instant onion
1/4 cup chopped parsley
Pinch of ground rosemary
4 tablespoons melted butter
1/2 cup boiling water

MINT SAUCE
1/2 cup water
1 teaspoon cider vinegar
1 tablespoon dried mint or 2 tablespoons fresh mint,
    chopped
1/2 cup red currant jelly
1/2 cup mint jelly

Sprinkle lamb chops with salt and pepper. In a bowl, mix the stuffing, onion, parsley, and rosemary; stir in butter and boiling water, tossing lightly with a fork.

In a shallow baking pan arrange lamb chops, bone side out, standing in a circle, filling the spaces between the chops with stuffing. Place the remainder of the stuffing inside the circle of chops. Loosely tie the chops and stuffing around the outside of the circle using string. Cover stuffing with aluminum foil and bake at 325°F for 1 hour.

Meanwhile, prepare Mint Sauce. Combine sauce ingredients in a saucepan and stir over low heat until smooth. Uncover lamb and bake 15 minutes longer, basting several times with mint sauce.
MAKES 6 TO 8 SERVINGS.

Poultry

Chicken and Stuffing à la Waldorf

1 apple, cored and chopped
1/2 cup chopped celery and leaves
1/2 cup butter or margarine
1 package (8 ounces) Herb Seasoned Stuffing
1/4 cup chopped pecans
1/4 cup raisins
1 teaspoon grated orange peel
1/4 teaspoon salt
1 cup water or broth
8 chicken breast quarters with wings
Salt and pepper to taste
8 bacon slices

Sauté apple and celery in butter until tender. Stir in next 6 ingredients and blend well. Spread evenly in a greased 9 x 13 x 2-inch baking dish. Top with chicken breasts. Sprinkle with salt and pepper. Top with bacon slices. Bake at 350°F for 40 to 45 minutes.
MAKES 8 SERVINGS.

Chicken in Cheese Sauce

1 package (10 ounces) frozen Bake It Fresh
    Patty Shells
1 cup sliced celery
1/2 cup sliced carrots
1/4 cup butter or margarine
1 can (10-3/4 ounces) condensed cream of
    chicken soup
1 can (11 ounces) condensed Cheddar cheese soup
1/2 cup milk
1/2 teaspoon onion salt
1 teaspoon paprika
Salt and pepper to taste
2 cups cooked boned chicken

Prepare Patty Shells as directed on package. In a saucepan, sauté celery and carrots in butter or margarine until tender. Add soups, milk, onion salt, paprika, salt, and pepper to taste. Mix thoroughly and stir in chicken. Simmer for about 15 minutes. Spoon into Patty Shells and serve immediately.
MAKES 4 SERVINGS.

Thighs With Stuffing Orientale

12 chicken thighs
Salt and pepper to taste
1/2 cup chopped onion
1/2 cup chopped celery
1/3 cup butter or margarine
1 cup water or chicken broth mixed with 1/4 cup
    soy sauce
1 package (8 ounces) Herb Seasoned Stuffing
1 can (6 ounces) water chestnuts, drained and sliced
1 cup catsup
1 cup pineapple juice

Remove bones from thighs by cutting along the thigh bones on either side with the tip of a sharp knife. Cut meat off ends of bones and remove bones. Sprinkle with salt and pepper; set aside. In a saucepan, sauté onion and celery in butter until tender. Stir in water mixture, stuffing, and water chestnuts. Toss lightly. Use mixture to stuff thighs and fasten with toothpicks. Place side by side in a shallow baking pan. Top with catsup mixed with pineapple juice. Bake at 350°F for 1 hour, basting with pan juices every 15 minutes.
MAKES 6 SERVINGS.

Sunday Brunch Puffs

1 package (10 ounces) frozen Bake It Fresh Patty Shells
3 tablespoons butter or margarine
3 tablespoons flour
1-1/2 cups milk
1/2 teaspoon salt
1 teaspoon Worcestershire sauce
2 cups cooked diced chicken, duck, or turkey
1/2 cup sliced stuffed olives
2 tablespoons chopped parsley

Prepare Patty Shells according to package directions. In a saucepan, melt butter or margarine; blend in flour. Gradually stir in milk, and cook over low heat, stirring constantly, until mixture thickens. Stir in remaining ingredients. Heat thoroughly, about 5 minutes. Spoon into warm Patty Shells and garnish with parsley.
MAKES 6 SERVINGS.

Sweet-Sour Turkey and Banana Bake

1/2 cup catsup
1 tablespoon prepared mustard
1 tablespoon Worcestershire sauce
1/4 cup water
1 cup sliced celery
1 medium green pepper, sliced
1 can (1 pound, 4 ounces) pineapple chunks in juice,
    undrained
4 cups diced cooked turkey
3 bananas
2 cups Herb Seasoned Stuffing

In a large bowl, mix catsup, mustard, Worcestershire sauce, and water. Stir in celery, green pepper, pineapple chunks with juice, and turkey. Peel and slice bananas; add to turkey mixture. Pour into a greased 3-quart casserole. Bake at 350°F for 25 minutes. Sprinkle casserole with stuffing and bake 15 minutes longer or until hot and bubbly.
MAKES 8 SERVINGS.

Game Hens With Oyster Stuffing

1 pint drained and chopped oysters or clams,
    reserve the liquid
1/4 cup chopped onion
1/4 cup chopped celery
1/2 cup melted butter or margarine
1 package (8 ounces) Herb Seasoned Stuffing
1/4 teaspoon poultry seasoning
Salt and pepper to taste
1/2 cup water
8 game hens (about 1 pound each), thawed
    if frozen
1/2 cup melted butter or margarine

Sauté oysters, onion, and celery in melted butter. Remove from heat. Stir in oyster liquid, stuffing, and seasonings; toss lightly. Add water as needed to moisten. Wash game hens with cold water and pat dry. Sprinkle game hens inside and out with salt and pepper. Stuff body and neck cavities of hens and sew or skewer openings. Brush with melted butter or margarine. Roast at 350°F for 1 hour, or until legs can be moved up and down easily.
MAKES 8 SERVINGS.

Danish Prune Stuffed Duckling

1/2 cup butter or margarine
1/2 cup chopped onion
1/2 cup chopped celery
Liver and heart from duckling, chopped
1-1/2 cups pitted quartered prunes
1 cup water
1/4 teaspoon ground cloves
1/4 teaspoon mace
1/8 teaspoon nutmeg
1 package (8 ounces) Herb Seasoned Stuffing
1 duckling (thawed, if frozen)
Salt and pepper to taste

Heat butter in a large saucepan and sauté the onion, celery, liver, and heart until just tender. Stir in prunes, water, and seasonings. Add stuffing and toss to blend. Wash and dry duckling. Stuff duckling and sew or skewer openings. Place remaining stuffing in a small 1-quart greased casserole. Prick duckling skin with a fork and set on a rack in a shallow pan. Roast at 350°F for 2 hours. Remove fat from time to time during roasting. Cover stuffing casserole; place in oven and bake for only 45 minutes.
MAKES 4 SERVINGS.

Ducklings With Sumptuous Fruit Stuffing

1/2 cup sliced green onion
1/2 cup (1 stick) butter or margarine
1-1/4 cups hot water
2 oranges, peeled and cut-up
1/2 cup halved seedless green grapes
1/3 cup coarsely chopped walnuts
1 egg, slightly beaten
1 package (8 ounces) Corn Bread Stuffing
2 ducklings (each 4 pounds), thawed if frozen
Salt and pepper to taste

In a saucepan, sauté onion in butter until tender. Add water, oranges, grapes, nuts, and egg. Combine with Corn Bread Stuffing and blend well. Wash and dry ducklings. Season insides. Stuff body cavities and sew or skewer openings. Prick skin with a fork and set on a rack in a shallow pan. Roast at 350°F for 2 hours. Remove fat from time to time during roasting.
MAKES 8 SERVINGS.

Turkey Breast With Sweet Potato Herb Stuffing

2 packages (8 ounces each) frozen raw turkey breast
        slices, thawed (12 large slices)
Salt and pepper to taste
1/2 pound sausage meat
1/4 cup chopped onion
1/4 cup chopped celery
1/2 cup butter or margarine
1 can (1 pound) golden yams (about 1-1/4 cups),
        drained and mashed
1/2 teaspoon grated orange peel
2 tablespoons chopped parsley
3/4 cup orange juice
1 egg, beaten
1 package (7 ounces) Cube Stuffing
1 can (10-3/4 ounces) condensed cream of
        mushroom soup, mixed with 1/3 cup milk

Sprinkle turkey with salt and pepper. Brown sausage, remove from fat, and drain on absorbent paper; discard sausage drippings. Sauté onion and celery in butter until tender. Stir in yams, orange peel, parsley, and cooked sausage. Stir in orange juice, egg, and stuffing; blend well. Spoon mixture on turkey slices and roll up. Secure with toothpicks. Place rolls side by side in a greased shallow baking dish. Top with soup mixture. Bake at 350°F for 1 hour.
MAKES 6 SERVINGS.

Chicken Livers Madeira

1 pound chicken livers, cut into quarters
2 tablespoons butter
1/4 cup Madeira wine
1 cup condensed chicken broth mixed with
        1 tablespoon cornstarch
English Muffins or Whole Wheat Bread

Sauté livers in butter until brown. Stir in Madeira wine and chicken broth mixture. Cook, stirring until thick and smooth. Simmer until livers are tender, about 5 minutes. Spoon over toasted English Muffins or triangles of toasted Whole Wheat Bread.
MAKES 4 SERVINGS.

Wash goose inside and out. Season cavity with salt and pepper. Pack stuffing lightly into cavity; sew or skewer opening. Prick skin with a fork. Place on a rack in a roasting pan and roast at 325°F for 3 hours. MAKES 6 SERVINGS.

Chicken in a Stuffing Nest

3 tablespoons butter or margarine
1/4 cup flour
1-1/2 cups chicken broth
1/2 cup light cream
2 cups diced cooked chicken or turkey
1 cup cooked peas
2/3 cup shredded carrots
1/2 cup chopped green onion
1/4 teaspoon thyme
1/8 teaspoon sage
Salt to taste
1 package (8 ounces) Herb Seasoned Stuffing
1/2 cup butter or margarine
1 cup boiling water

In a saucepan, melt butter. Stir in flour until smooth. Remove from heat. Gradually stir in chicken broth and cream; heat, stirring until thickened and smooth. Fold in chicken, peas, carrots, onion, thyme, and sage. Add salt to taste. Prepare stuffing according to package directions using butter and water. Press stuffing against sides and bottom of greased 1-1/2-quart baking dish. Pour hot chicken mixture into center of prepared dish. Bake at 400°F for 20 to 25 minutes, or until hot and bubbly. MAKES 4 SERVINGS.

Chicken Stuffed With Apricot Sausage Corn Bread

1 pound bulk sausage
1-1/2 cups chopped onion
1/2 cup chopped celery
1/2 cup apple juice or water
1 package (8 ounces) Corn Bread Stuffing
1-1/2 cups chopped pecans or walnuts
1/4 cup chopped parsley
2 cans (17 ounces each) apricot halves or
    peach slices, juice reserved
1 chicken, about 6 pounds
Salt and pepper to taste
Juice of 1 lemon

In a large skillet, break up sausage and cook until browned. Add onion and celery, cook until tender. Add apple juice, bring to a boil. Add stuffing, nuts, parsley, and apricots; mix lightly. Wash chicken and pat dry. Sprinkle chicken with salt and pepper. Stuff body and neck cavities and sew or skewer openings. Pack remaining stuffing in a small, greased casserole. Roast chicken at 350°F for 2 hours, or until leg can be moved up and down easily. Bake casserole 30 minutes, or until hot. Mix reserved apricot juice and lemon juice. Brush chicken with juice every 15 minutes during roasting.
MAKES 6 TO 8 SERVINGS.

Fruited Stuffed Goose

6 slices bacon
1/2 cup chopped green onion
1/4 cup chopped green pepper
1 package (8 ounces) Herb Seasoned Stuffing
1-1/4 cups water
1 cup diced peaches
1/2 cup chopped dates
1 egg, slightly beaten
1 goose (about 8 pounds), thawed if frozen
1 teaspoon salt
1/8 teaspoon pepper

In a skillet, cook bacon until crisp. Remove and crumble; set aside. Add onion and green pepper to drippings; cook until tender. Combine stuffing, bacon, vegetables, water, peaches, dates, and egg. Blend well.

Sesame-Parsley Stuffed Chicken Breasts

6 whole chicken breasts, skinned and boned
Salt and pepper to taste
1/2 cup butter or margarine
2 tablespoons sesame seeds
3/4 cup finely chopped parsley
1 cup water
1 package (7 ounces) Cube Stuffing
1 jar (4 ounces) pimientos, drained and chopped
1/2 cup melted butter or margarine

Pound chicken until 1/4-inch thick. Sprinkle with salt and pepper. Melt butter in large saucepan. Add sesame seeds and sauté lightly. Add parsley and sauté 1 minute. Stir in water, then add stuffing and pimientos; toss until blended. Spoon stuffing on chicken breasts. Roll up to enclose fillings; fasten with a toothpick. Spread half of the melted butter in a shallow 9 x 13 x 2-inch baking dish. Top with chicken. Drizzle with remaining butter. Bake at 350°F for 40 to 50 minutes. Serve with your favorite tomato or mushroom sauce, or serve garnished with orange slices.
MAKES 6 SERVINGS.

Stuffing Ring With Turkey à la King

1 package (8 ounces) Herb Seasoned Stuffing
1 can (10-3/4 ounces) condensed chicken broth
4 eggs, well beaten
1 cup milk
2 cans (10-3/4 ounces each) condensed cream of
    chicken soup
2 cups diced cooked turkey
1 jar (4 ounces) pimiento, drained and diced
1 package (10 ounces) frozen peas

In a bowl, mix stuffing, chicken broth, eggs, and milk. Pour mixture into a well-greased 6-cup ring mold. Bake at 350°F for about 40 minutes, or until puffed and brown. While ring is baking, combine remaining ingredients in a saucepan and simmer until piping hot and peas are cooked. Unmold ring on a platter and pour Turkey à la King into a bowl and place in center of ring. When serving, cut ring into slices and spoon Turkey à la King over stuffing.
MAKES 6 SERVINGS.

Pineapple-Lime-Chicken Mold

1 can (1 pound, 4 ounces) pineapple chunks
Water
2 packages (3 ounces each) lime gelatin
1 cup mayonnaise
1 cup (1/2 pint) sour cream
2 cups diced cooked chicken or turkey
1 cup chopped celery and leaves
Lettuce leaves
Sprouted Wheat Bread

Drain syrup from pineapple chunks; add enough water to the syrup to make 2 cups. Heat mixture to boiling and stir in gelatin to dissolve. Beat in mayonnaise and sour cream. Chill until gelatin is slightly thickened. Fold pineapple, chicken or turkey, and celery into gelatin. Pour mixture into a lightly oiled (9 x 5 x 3-inch) 2-quart loaf pan or mold and chill until firm. Unmold and invert onto a serving platter which has been lined with lettuce leaves. To serve, cut into slices. Serve with slices of Sprouted Wheat Bread.
MAKES 6 SERVINGS.

Herbed Chicken Vegetable Casserole

1 can (10-3/4 ounces) condensed cream of
    celery soup
1-1/2 cups milk
2 tablespoons minced onion
Salt and pepper to taste
1/2 teaspoon crumbled dried basil
2 cups cooked and drained elbow macaroni
2-1/2 cups diced cooked leftover chicken
    or turkey
2 packages (10 ounces each) frozen Japanese-
    style vegetables, thawed
1 package (6 ounces) Onion & Garlic Croutons

In a 2-quart casserole, combine soup, milk, onion, salt, pepper, and basil. Mix well and stir in macaroni, chicken, and thawed vegetables. Add any seasoning included in vegetable package. Cover and bake at 350°F for 20 minutes. Sprinkle croutons over chicken mixture and continue baking uncovered, for 5 more minutes.
MAKES 6 SERVINGS.

Giblet Gravy

Turkey heart
Turkey liver
Turkey neck
Turkey gizzard
Water
1 teaspoon salt
1/4 teaspoon pepper
1 small onion, sliced
1 celery rib, chopped
1/3 cup flour

Place turkey heart, liver, neck, and gizzard in saucepan and cover with water. Add salt, pepper, onion, and celery. Cover and simmer 1 to 1-1/2 hours, until tender, adding water to keep up the level of the liquid, when necessary. Strain broth and dice cooked parts or giblets. To make gravy, remove turkey from roasting pan to platter; remove rack. Skim most of fat from pan juices. To juices in pan, add giblet broth and enough water to make 3 cups. Add diced giblets. Bring to a boil, stirring brown crustiness from bottom of pan. To thicken gravy, stir flour into enough water to make a thin smooth paste, and stir into pan juices. Cook, stirring constantly, until gravy thickens and is smooth. Season to taste with salt and pepper.
MAKES ABOUT 3 CUPS.

Pan-Style Baked Chicken

1 3-pound broiler-fryer, cut up
Salt and pepper to taste
1/4 cup butter or margarine
1 package (6 ounces) Chicken & Herb Pan
    Style Stuffing
2-1/2 cups milk
3 eggs, slightly beaten

Wash chicken and pat dry. Sprinkle chicken with salt and pepper. In a large skillet, brown chicken pieces in butter. Remove; set aside. Mix pan drippings with stuffing, milk, and eggs; blend well. Place stuffing mixture in a greased 2-quart shallow casserole. Place browned chicken pieces in a single layer over top of stuffing. Bake at 350°F for 1 hour.
MAKES 6 SERVINGS.

Roast Turkey With Banana Pecan Herb Stuffing

1/2 cup butter or margarine
1/2 cup finely chopped onion
1 cup (1/2 pint) light cream
1 package (8 ounces) Herb Seasoned Stuffing
1 cup chopped pecans
1-1/2 cups (3 medium) diced bananas

1 turkey (about 12 pounds)
1 tablespoon salt
1/2 teaspoon pepper
1 cup water

2/3 cup (2 medium) mashed bananas
1/4 cup orange juice
1/2 cup currant jelly
2 tablespoons lemon juice

Giblet Gravy

In a large skillet, melt butter; add onion and cook until tender. Add cream and remove from heat. Add stuffing and pecans; mix well. Peel and dice bananas; add to stuffing.

Rinse turkey inside and out under cold running water; dry. Sprinkle body and neck cavities with salt and pepper and stuff lightly. Sew or skewer openings. Place turkey breast side up on a rack in a shallow roasting pan and add water. Bake at 325°F for 3-1/4 hours.

Meanwhile, combine bananas and remaining ingredients in small saucepan; heat until jelly melts. Brush glaze on turkey and bake 30 to 45 minutes longer, basting frequently. Allow to stand 20 to 30 minutes before carving. If desired, serve with Giblet Gravy (see page 57).
MAKES 10 TO 12 SERVINGS.

Holiday Game Hens

1 cup chopped onions
1 cup sliced mushrooms
1/2 cup chopped pecans
1/2 cup butter or margarine
1 cup water
1 package (7 ounces) Cube Stuffing
1-1/2 cups cranberries
3 tablespoons sugar
1/2 cup chopped parsley
Grated peel of 1 orange
6 game hens (about 1 pound each), thawed
     if frozen
Salt and pepper to taste
1/2 cup marmalade mixed with 1/4 cup
     soy sauce

In a large saucepan, sauté onions, mushrooms, and pecans in butter for 5 minutes. Add water, bring to a boil. Stir in stuffing, cranberries, sugar, parsley, and orange peel, stirring to blend. Wash and dry game hens; sprinkle with salt and pepper. Stuff hens and sew or skewer openings. Roast at 350°F for 45 minutes. Spread with marmalade mixture and roast another 15 minutes, or until legs can be moved up and down easily.
MAKES 6 SERVINGS.

Mushroom Stuffing Cups

1/2 cup chopped onion
1/2 cup chopped celery
1 cup sliced mushrooms
1/3 cup butter or margarine
1 cup chicken broth
1 package (7 ounces) Herb Seasoned Stuffing
1 egg
1 tablespoon chopped parsley
Salt and pepper to taste

Sauté onions, celery, and mushrooms in butter. Stir in broth; bring to boiling. Remove from heat. Add stuffing, egg, parsley, salt, and pepper. Toss lightly. Place in heavily greased custard cups. Bake at 350°F for 20 to 30 minutes. Muffin tins can also be used.
MAKES 12 CUPS.

Serve poultry or other roasts with stuffing made in many shapes
Stuffing Balls: Form stuffing into balls with an ice cream dipper or 1/3 cup measure. Place on a greased cookie sheet and bake at 350°F for 20 to 30 minutes.

Stuffing Sticks: Place stuffing on greased baking sheet and press into rectangular shape about 1 inch thick and 6 inches wide. Bake at 350°F for 20 to 30 minutes. Cut into 6 bars.

Stuffing Squares: Place stuffing in greased 8-inch square pan and spread evenly with a spatula. Bake at 350°F for 20 to 30 minutes. Cut into 6 squares.
MAKES 6 SERVINGS.

Oven Fried Chicken With Cream Gravy

2 cups Herb Seasoned Stuffing, crushed
   very fine
1 teaspoon salt
1 egg
1 tablespoon water
1 chicken (about 3 pounds), cut-up
1/4 cup butter or margarine

1 can (10-1/2 ounces) chicken gravy
1/2 cup sour cream

Combine crushed stuffing and salt in a plastic bag. Beat egg with water. Dip chicken parts into egg mixture, then shake, a few pieces at a time, in bag until well coated with stuffing. Melt butter in a shallow baking pan. Place chicken, skin side down, in melted butter in a single layer. Bake uncovered at 350°F for 30 minutes; turn chicken and continue baking for 15 minutes.

   In a saucepan, mix gravy with sour cream. Heat until hot, but do not boil. Serve over chicken.
MAKES 4 SERVINGS.

Turkey Cantonese

1/4 cup butter or margarine
3/4 cup chopped onion
1 cup sliced celery
1 cup thinly sliced raw carrots
1 teaspoon cornstarch
1/4 teaspoon ginger
1 can (10-3/4 ounces) condensed cream of chicken soup
3/4 cup water
1 tablespoon soy sauce
1 teaspoon lemon juice
1 cup drained pineapple tidbits
2 cups cooked diced turkey
1 can (5 ounces) water chestnuts, drained and
    thinly sliced
6 Sourdough English Muffins

In a large skillet, melt butter or margarine; sauté onions, celery, and carrots until crisp and golden. Combine cornstarch, ginger, cream of chicken soup, water, soy sauce, and lemon juice; mix until well blended. Add to sautéed vegetables and simmer over low heat until mixture thickens slightly, stirring constantly. Stir in pineapple tidbits, turkey, and water chestnuts; cover, simmer 10 to 15 minutes. Serve spooned over split and toasted Sourdough English Muffins.
MAKES 6 SERVINGS.

Chinese Chicken Wings With Apricot-Almond Stuffing Mold

24 chicken wings
Salt and pepper to taste
1/3 cup honey
1/3 cup soy sauce
1/2 teaspoon garlic powder
1 cup dried apricots, cut into strips
1 cup water
1 tablespoon brown sugar
1 tablespoon lemon juice
1/2 cup butter or margarine
1 package (7 ounces) Cube Stuffing
1/2 cup slivered almonds
1/4 teaspoon salt

Sprinkle chicken wings with salt and pepper. Brush with honey mixed with soy sauce and garlic powder. Place in a single layer in a large, greased, foil-lined pan.

Simmer apricots, water, brown sugar, and lemon juice in a small saucepan for 5 minutes. Drain and add enough water to reserved liquid to make 1 cup. Place liquid in large saucepan with butter and heat until butter is melted. Stir in stuffing, apricots, almonds, and salt. Pack mixture into a heavily greased 1-1/2-quart mold or heatproof bowl. Cover and bake wings and stuffing separately at 350°F for 40 to 45 minutes. Unmold stuffing onto serving platter; surround by chicken wings.
MAKES 6 SERVINGS.

Chicken Divan

1 package (10 ounces) frozen Bake It Fresh
    Patty Shells
1 can (10-3/4 ounces) condensed cream of
    chicken soup
1 can (10-3/4 ounces) condensed cream of
    mushroom soup
1/2 cup milk
1-1/2 cups diced cooked chicken
1 cup diced cooked broccoli
1/4 cup grated Parmesan cheese

Bake Patty Shells as directed on package. Meanwhile, in a saucepan, combine and heat condensed soups and milk. Stir in chicken and broccoli. Heat until mixture starts to bubble. Spoon into baked Patty Shells. Sprinkle with cheese.
MAKES 4 TO 6 SERVINGS.

Sea Food

Cod in a Crust

1/4 cup minced onion
3 tablespoons butter or margarine
1/4 cup flour
1 can (10-3/4 ounces) condensed cream of shrimp soup
1 cup milk
3 cups flaked, cooked codfish
Several drops of tabasco sauce
1 package (10 ounces) chopped broccoli, thawed
    and drained
1 package (12 ounces) Large Sandwich Pockets
Tomatoes
Parsley

In a saucepan, sauté onion in butter until soft, but not brown. Add flour and cook, stirring until bubbly. Mix in soup and milk. Heat, stirring constantly, until mixture is smooth. Fold in fish, tabasco, and broccoli, and simmer until bubbly. Cut Sandwich Pockets into halves. Spoon fish mixture into Pockets. Garnish with tomato wedges and parsley.
MAKES 4 GENEROUS SERVINGS.

Red Snapper Diablo

1/3 cup butter or margarine
1 clove garlic, chopped
1/3 cup flour
2 cups tomato juice
4 cups cooked flaked red snapper or other firm
    white fish
1 can (4 ounces) whole button mushrooms, drained
1/2 cup dry sherry
1/4 cup lemon juice
1/2 teaspoon salt
1 tablespoon Worcestershire sauce
English Muffins, split and toasted

In a chafing dish or skillet, melt butter and sauté garlic. Stir in flour. Gradually stir in tomato juice. Cook slowly, stirring constantly until sauce thickens. Fold in red snapper pieces, mushrooms, sherry, lemon juice, salt, and Worcestershire sauce. To serve, spoon over split, toasted English Muffins. Serve with a crisp watercress, endive, and tomato salad.
MAKES 6 SERVINGS.

Egg Scallop Scramble

2 tablespoons butter or margarine
1 pound fresh or thawed frozen bay scallops
6 beaten eggs
1/3 cup light cream
1/2 teaspoon salt
Dash of pepper
Snipped parsley
4 to 6 slices Sprouted Wheat Bread, toasted

In a skillet, melt butter. Add scallops and simmer until golden. Beat eggs with light cream, salt, and pepper to taste. Pour over scallops. Cook over low heat, stirring until cooked but not dry. Fold in parsley. Spoon over toasted bread slices. Serve with broiled tomato halves.
MAKES 4 TO 6 SERVINGS.

Note: If using sea scallops, cut each scallop into 2 to 3 pieces.

Brunch Scallop Kabobs

2 pounds large sea scallops
12 mushroom caps
12 cherry tomatoes
3 green peppers, cut into 1-1/2-inch squares
3 red peppers, cut into 1-1/2-inch squares
1/2 cup melted butter or margarine
1 tablespoon chopped chives
1/2 teaspoon salt
Dash of garlic powder
6 cups mashed cooked butternut squash
1/3 cup melted butter or margarine
1/2 cup pineapple juice
Salt to taste
Butter Crescent Rolls

On heatproof skewers, spear scallops, mushrooms, tomatoes, and peppers. Mix butter, chives, salt, and garlic powder. Brush mixture over kabobs. Place under broiler and broil until golden, about 4 to 5 minutes; turn and broil for another 4 to 5 minutes. Mix squash with butter and pineapple juice. Add salt to taste and heat until piping hot. Spoon squash on serving dishes and top with kabobs. Serve with Butter Crescent Rolls.
MAKES 6 SERVINGS.

Stuffed Bass

2-pound whole bass, cleaned and scaled
Salt and pepper to taste
1/4 cup butter or margarine
6 scallions or 1 onion, chopped
4 slices Sprouted Wheat Bread, crumbled
3 hard-cooked eggs, chopped
**1 package (6 ounces) frozen king crab meat, thawed
    and drained**
2 tablespoons chopped parsley
1/2 cup tartar sauce
1/4 cup dry white wine
1/3 cup melted butter
Juice of 1 lemon
1 onion, sliced

Sprinkle bass inside and out with salt and pepper. If necessary, cut fish inside along the backbone to make a larger pocket. In a skillet, melt butter and sauté scallions for 2 to 3 minutes. Stir in bread, eggs, crab meat, parsley, tartar sauce, and wine. Use mixture to stuff bass. Close opening with toothpicks. Place fish on a greased shallow baking pan. Brush with butter mixed with lemon juice. Top with onion slices. Bake at 350°F for 40 to 45 minutes, or until fish flakes easily. Serve topped with your favorite mushroom sauce.
MAKES 4 TO 6 SERVINGS.

Tuna Tetrazzini Goldfish Casserole

1 can (10-3/4 ounces) condensed cream of chicken soup
1/4 cup dry sherry
1/4 cup sour cream
1 can (7 ounces) tuna, drained and flaked
1 can (6 ounces) sliced mushrooms, drained
3 cups cooked drained spaghetti
1 cup Cheddar Cheese Goldfish or any flavor croutons

In a bowl, mix soup, sherry, sour cream, tuna, and mushrooms. Place spaghetti into a shallow 1-1/2-quart casserole. Spoon tuna mixture evenly over spaghetti. Sprinkle with Goldfish or croutons. Bake at 350°F for 30 to 35 minutes, or until hot and bubbly. Serve with a tossed green salad.
MAKES 2 GENEROUS SERVINGS.

Shrimp Boats With Lemon Sails

4 cups shelled and deveined cooked shrimp
    (1-1/2 pounds)
1 cup diced celery
4 hard-cooked eggs, chopped
1/3 cup sliced green onions
1/4 cup chopped dill pickle
1 cup mayonnaise or salad dressing
2 tablespoons chili sauce
2 teaspoons horseradish
1 teaspoon salt
2 packages (8 ounces each) Brown-and-Serve Club Rolls
Melted butter
Lettuce leaves
Lemon slices

Cut up shrimp, reserving 12 shrimp for garnish. Combine shrimp, celery, eggs, onions, and dill pickle. Fold in mayonnaise, chili sauce, horseradish, and salt. Chill.

Bake Brown-and-Serve Club Rolls according to package directions. Cut a thin slice off the top of the roll and scoop out the inside. Brush with melted butter. Line roll "boat" with lettuce; mound with shrimp salad. To trim, thread reserved whole shrimp and twists of lemon slices (to resemble sails) on toothpicks. Place in salad; garnish with parsley.

Makes 12 shrimp boats.

Baked Haddock

2 packages (1 pound each) frozen haddock fillets
1 cup mayonnaise
2 tablespoons prepared mustard
1 tablespoon Worcestershire sauce
4 slices Pumpernickel Bread, crumbled
1/4 cup melted butter or margarine

With a sharp serrated knife, cut each frozen fillet into 3 pieces. Place pieces side by side in a greased shallow casserole. In a bowl, mix mayonnaise, mustard, and Worcestershire sauce. Spread mixture over the top of the fish pieces. Mix bread crumbs with butter and sprinkle over fish. Bake at 350°F for 30 to 35 minutes, or until fish is cooked and flakes easily.

Makes 6 servings.

Coquilles St. Jacques

1/3 cup butter or margarine
1/3 cup flour
1/2 cup chicken broth
1/2 cup dry white wine
1 cup (1/2 pint) heavy cream
1 can (6 ounces) sliced mushrooms, drained
1 pound shrimp, cooked, shelled and deveined
1 pound scallops, cooked
Salt and pepper to taste
1 cup Cheese Snack Sticks, crushed

In a saucepan, melt butter and stir in flour. Gradually stir in chicken broth, wine, and cream. Stir over low heat until sauce thickens and bubbles; continue stirring for 2 to 3 minutes. Fold in mushrooms, shrimp, and scallops, and season to taste with salt and pepper. Spoon mixture into individual casseroles, or into an 8-inch square baking pan. Sprinkle top with crushed Snack Sticks. Bake at 350°F for 25 to 30 minutes, or until browned and bubbly.
MAKES 6 SERVINGS.

Note: Shrimp and scallops may be cooked by covering with water and heating until water comes to a boil. Drain. For variation, omit shrimp and substitute scallops using 2 pounds scallops, or use 3 cups large chunks cooked firm fish such as cod, flounder, haddock, halibut, or salmon.

Haddock and Almond Quiche

1/4 cup butter or margarine
1/3 cup sliced almonds
1 pound fresh or frozen halibut or other white fish
  fillets, cut into 1 inch cubes
1-1/2 cups (6 ounces) grated Swiss cheese
1 tablespoon flour
2 frozen Pie Shells, thawed
4 eggs
2 cups (1 pint) half and half
1 teaspoon salt
1/2 teaspoon dill weed

*Haddock and Almond Quiche
and Coquilles St. Jacques*

In a skillet, heat butter and sauté almonds until golden brown. If using frozen fish, do not thaw but cut with a serrated knife. Add fish and continue cooking until fish becomes white and flakes easily. Mix cheese with flour and sprinkle evenly in pie shells. Top with a layer of fish and almonds.

In a bowl, beat eggs with half and half, salt and dill. Divide mixture evenly between 2 pie shells. Bake both pies in a preheated moderate oven (350°) for 40 to 50 minutes or until puffed and richly browned. Let stand 10 minutes before cutting.
EACH PIE MAKES 6 SERVINGS.

NOTE: If desired, bake only 1 pie now and freeze the second pie unbaked for future use. Bake frozen pie at 325° for 45-50 minutes. To use frozen pie shells in quiche pans, thaw only a few minutes or until pie shells are loosened from the foil pan. Lift them carefully by the edges and transfer into the same size quiche pans. Allow shells to thaw 20 to 25 minutes or until soft. Press pie crusts firmly against the bottom and sides of quiche pans. If any cracks, press edges of dough together until cracks disappear.

Crab Stuffed Green Peppers

4 large whole green peppers
1/4 cup diced celery
1/4 cup minced onion
1/2 cup butter or margarine
1/2 cup water
1/4 cup lemon juice
1 can (6 ounces) crab meat, undrained
1 package (8 ounces) Herb Seasoned Stuffing

Cut off tops of peppers and remove seeds. Place peppers in enough boiling salted water to cover. Reduce heat and simmer 8 minutes. Drain.

In a saucepan, sauté celery and onion in butter. Stir in water, lemon juice, crab meat, juices from crab meat, and stuffing. Spoon mixture into peppers. Arrange peppers in buttered deep casserole and bake at 350°F for about 30 minutes, keeping peppers covered loosely with foil for first 15 minutes. Remove foil for last 15 minutes. Serve with your favorite cheese or tomato sauce.
MAKES 4 SERVINGS.

Seafood Strata

8 slices Wheat Germ Bread
1 cup (4 ounces) shredded Swiss cheese
1 can (7 ounces) tuna or salmon, drained and flaked
1/4 cup chopped onion
1/4 cup chopped green pepper
2 tablespoons butter or margarine
2 cups milk
2 eggs, slightly beaten
3/4 teaspoon salt
1/4 teaspoon chili powder

Alternate layers of bread, cheese, and tuna in well-buttered 9-inch square baking dish, beginning with bread and ending with cheese. In small saucepan, cook onion and green pepper in butter until vegetables are tender. Remove from heat and stir in milk, eggs, salt, and chili powder. Pour mixture evenly over ingredients in baking dish. Cover and let stand at room temperature at least 30 minutes to allow bread to absorb custard mixture. Bake at 350°F for 40 minutes, or until puffy and lightly browned.
MAKES 4 TO 6 SERVINGS.

Halibut and Broccoli au Gratin on Toasted Rolls

1/3 cup butter or margarine
1/3 cup flour
2 cups milk
1 cup (4 ounces) grated sharp Cheddar cheese
1 teaspoon dry mustard
3 cups cooked flaked halibut pieces (can be leftover
    cooked fish)
1 bunch broccoli, trimmed, cooked, and cut into
    bite-size pieces
Salt and pepper to taste
Plain or Sourdough English Muffins, split and toasted
Paprika for garnish

In a saucepan, melt butter and stir in flour. Gradually blend in milk. Stir over medium heat until sauce thickens and bubbles. Stir in cheese and mustard. Fold in halibut and broccoli. Season to taste with salt and pepper. To serve, spoon halibut and broccoli mixture over split toasted muffins and sprinkle with paprika.
MAKES 6 GENEROUS SERVINGS.

Salmon Provençale

6 salmon steaks
Salt and pepper to taste
2 tablespoons butter
1 small onion, finely chopped
1 clove garlic, minced
1 can (6 ounces) sliced mushrooms, drained
1/4 teaspoon thyme
2 tablespoons flour
1 can (16 ounces) stewed tomatoes
1/2 cup dry white wine
2 tablespoons chopped parsley

Sprinkle steaks with salt and pepper. Broil or poach salmon as desired until cooked. Meanwhile, in a large saucepan, heat butter and sauté onion and garlic for 5 minutes, until golden brown. Stir in mushrooms, thyme, and flour. Gradually stir in tomatoes and wine. Stir over medium heat until sauce bubbles and thickens. Simmer 5 minutes. Stir in parsley. Season to taste with salt and pepper. Spoon hot sauce over salmon steaks. Serve at once with Herbed Asparagus (see page 102).
MAKES 6 SERVINGS.

Note: Poached white fish steaks, such as cod, halibut, or fresh tuna, can be used also.

Corny Seafood Bake

2 pounds fish fillets
1 egg, well beaten
1 tablespoon water
1 package (8 ounces) Corn Bread Stuffing, rolled fine
    with a rolling pin, blender, or food processor
Salt and pepper to taste
1/4 cup melted butter or margarine

Any assortment of fish may be used. Cut fish into serving size pieces. Dip fish into beaten egg mixed with water and then roll in stuffing crumbs. Season with salt and pepper to taste. Place on heavily greased, foil-lined baking sheet, and drizzle with melted butter. Bake at 350°F for about 20 to 25 minutes. Serve with tartar sauce and cocktail sauce.
MAKES 6 SERVINGS.

Sprouted Wheat and Tuna Pie

2 packages (12 ounces each) frozen macaroni and cheese,
    thawed
2 cans (7 ounces each) tuna, drained and flaked
1 package (10 ounces) frozen peas in butter sauce, thawed
6 slices Sprouted Wheat Bread, cut into cubes
6 slices American cheese, diced

In a bowl, mix macaroni and cheese, tuna, and peas, and pour into a greased 1-1/2-quart casserole. Sprinkle top with bread and cheese. Bake at 350°F for 35 to 40 minutes, or until browned and bubbly.
MAKES 6 SERVINGS.

Salmon Stuffed Fillets With Rye Bread Sauce

6 large fresh flounder fillets, or frozen turbot fillets,
    thawed slightly
Salt and pepper to taste
1 can (7 ounces) salmon, drained, skin and bones
    removed
2 tablespoons drained capers
1 tablespoon each chopped scallions and parsley
2 slices Rye Bread, crumbled
1/2 cup melted butter or margarine

1/3 cup minced celery
2 slices Rye Bread, crumbled
1 cup chicken broth
1 cup (1/2 pint) light cream

Sprinkle flounder fillets with salt and pepper. In a bowl, mix salmon, capers, scallions, parsley, and crumbled bread. Dividing mixture equally, place stuffing at large end of fillets and roll up like a jelly roll; hold in place with toothpicks. Place rolls seam side down in a buttered shallow baking pan. Brush rolls with half of the butter. Bake at 350°F for 25 to 30 minutes, or until fish flakes easily.

Meanwhile in a saucepan, sauté celery in remaining butter. Stir in bread, chicken broth, and cream. Stir over low heat until sauce thickens and bubbles; simmer for 5 minutes stirring frequently. Season to taste with salt and pepper. Serve fillets with sauce.
MAKES 6 SERVINGS.

Goldfish Gala

1 pound raw shrimp, cooked, shelled and deveined or 1
    package (12 ounces) thawed, cooked frozen shrimp
4 cups cooked and diced turkey
1/4 cup butter or margarine
1/2 cup flour
2 cups (1 pint) milk
1/2 cup dry Sherry
1 can (6 ounces) sliced mushrooms, drained
1 package (10 ounces) frozen peas
Salt and pepper to taste
1 package (6 ounces) Parmesan Cheese Goldfish
    Crackers

Mix shrimp and turkey. In a saucepan, heat butter until melted. Stir in flour and gradually blend in milk and sherry. Stir over low heat until sauce bubbles and thickens. Fold in turkey, shrimp, mushrooms, and frozen peas; stir until peas separate. Season to taste with salt and pepper.

Pour mixture into greased 2-quart casserole and sprinkle top with an even layer of Goldfish Crackers. Cover casserole loosely with foil to prevent overbrowning Goldfish. Bake at 350°F for 30 to 35 minutes. MAKES 6 TO 8 SERVINGS.

Note: If casserole is to be refrigerated for several hours, top with Goldfish when ready to bake.

Crunchy Flounder Fillets

4 flounder fillets
1 can (1 pound) stewed tomatoes
1 cup Sour Cream & Chive Croutons
1/4 cup melted butter or margarine
1/2 teaspoon paprika
1/4 cup lemon juice
2 tablespoons chopped parsley

Place flounder fillets on broiler pan. Combine tomatoes and croutons. Top each fillet with 1/4 of the crouton mixture and fold fillets in half enclosing filling. Brush with melted butter mixed with paprika and lemon juice. Broil for 8 to 10 minutes, or until fish flakes easily and is cooked. Place on serving platter and sprinkle with chopped parsley. MAKES 4 SERVINGS.

Shrimps Mediterranean

1/2 cup olive oil
3 cloves garlic, minced
1 teaspoon salt
1/3 cup chopped parsley
2 pounds raw shrimp, shelled and deveined
1 can (6 ounces) chopped mushrooms
Water
1 package (8 ounces) Herb Seasoned Stuffing
1/2 cup melted butter or margarine
Grated Parmesan cheese
6 lemon wedges

Combine oil, garlic, salt, and parsley; sprinkle over shrimp. Refrigerate. Drain mushrooms, reserving liquid. Add enough water to liquid to make 1 cup. Stir this liquid into stuffing along with mushrooms and melted butter. Divide mixture between 6 scallop shells, or 6 individual casseroles. Top with shrimp and some of the oil mixture. Sprinkle with cheese. Bake at 350°F for 25 to 30 minutes, or until shrimp are pink and stuffing is piping hot. Serve with lemon wedges.
MAKES 6 SERVINGS.

Deviled Seafood

1/4 cup finely chopped green pepper
1/4 cup finely chopped onion
1 cup finely chopped celery
1 teaspoon Worcestershire sauce
1/2 teaspoon salt
1 can (6 to 7 ounces) shrimp, drained
1 can (6 to 7 ounces) flaked crab meat, drained
2 cups Herb Seasoned Stuffing, crushed after measuring
1 cup mayonnaise
1/2 cup milk

Stir together all ingredients until blended. Spoon into a 1-quart shallow casserole, or 8 ovenproof shells. Bake at 350°F for 30 minutes, or until browned.
MAKES 6 TO 8 SERVINGS.

Note: Omit shrimp and crab meat and substitute 2 cups flaked cooked fish such as halibut, haddock, cod, salmon, or flounder.

Salmon-Oatmeal Loaf

LOAF
2 cups cooked or canned salmon
2/3 cup evaporated milk
4 cups coarsely chopped Oatmeal Bread, about 8 slices
2 eggs, well beaten
2 tablespoons minced parsley
3 tablespoons minced onion
1/2 teaspoon salt
Dash of pepper
1/8 teaspoon sage

PIQUANT SAUCE
2 cups medium white sauce
1/2 cup mayonnaise
1/3 cup chopped almonds
1/3 cup stuffed olives

Combine salmon, milk, and bread; mix with a fork until well blended. Add eggs and remaining loaf ingredients; mix well. Put mixture into a well-greased (9 x 5 x 3-inch) loaf pan and bake at 375°F for about 40 minutes, or until center is firm. Cut loaf into slices and serve with piquant sauce.

To make sauce: Heat white sauce with mayonnaise, almonds, and olives until bubbly.
MAKES 6 SERVINGS.

Note: White sauce can be made using 1/4 cup butter or margarine, 1/4 cup flour, and 2 cups milk, cooked and seasoned to taste with salt and pepper.

Seafood Newburg Vol-au-Vent

1 package (17-1/4 ounces) frozen Bake It Fresh Puff Pastry
5 tablespoons butter or margarine
1 teaspoon paprika
1/4 cup flour
Juice from lobster meat plus milk to make 1 cup
1 pound fresh or frozen raw shrimp, cooked, shelled and deveined

1 can (14 ounces) lobster, reserve juice
1/2 cup dry sherry
1/2 teaspoon salt
Dash pepper

Thaw puff pastry 20 minutes, then unfold. Cut each puff pastry sheet in half. You will have 4 — 5 x 10 inch oblongs. Place 2 sheets of pastry side by side on a baking sheet. (One sheet will be baked for a lid and the other sheet will be topped with 2 pastry borders to shape a container for the Seafood Newburg.) With a sharp knife, cut out center of remaining 2 pastry sheets, leaving a border 1-inch wide. Place 2 borders on top of one of the sheets of pastry sealing them together with water. Cut pastry removed into 1-inch strips. Bake the shells and lid in a preheated hot oven (425°) for 35 to 40 minutes or until richly browned. Bake the strips only 12 to 15 minutes.

Melt butter in saucepan; stir in paprika and flour. Stir in milk and liquid drained from lobster. Bring to a boil over low heat, stirring constantly until mixture is thick. Fold in shrimp, lobster, sherry and salt. Season to taste with pepper. Reheat until bubbly. Place bottom of Vol-Au-Vent on a serving plate. Fill with shrimp mixture. Top with lid. Cut into serving-size pieces and serve with strips of pastry.
MAKES 8 SERVINGS.

NOTE: Instead of shrimp and lobster, substitute 1-1/2 pounds scallops or 1-1/2 pounds halibut cut into 1 inch cubes.

Rock Lobster Asparagus Newburg

1 package (10 ounces) frozen Bake It Fresh Patty Shells
2 frozen rock lobster tails (6 ounces each)
6 tablespoons butter
1/2 cup flour
1/2 teaspoon salt
1/4 teaspoon nutmeg
1/4 teaspoon pepper
2-1/2 cups milk
2 egg yolks, slightly beaten
2 tablespoons lemon juice
1 pound asparagus, trimmed, cut into 1-inch pieces
    and cooked
1 cup chopped cooked celery

Prepare Patty Shells according to package directions. Thaw lobster tails slightly in cold water. With scissors, remove underside membrane from raw lobster tails and pull out meat in one piece; cut into bite-size cubes. In a large skillet, sauté lobster in 3 tablespoons of the butter for about 3 minutes. Remove lobster and set aside. Add remaining butter to skillet and melt. Stir in flour and seasonings. Gradually stir in milk and cook until thick and smooth, stirring constantly. Fold a small amount of sauce into egg yolks. Gradually fold this mixture into remaining sauce. Stir in lemon juice, asparagus, celery, and rock lobster. Season to taste with salt and pepper. Heat thoroughly and spoon into warm Patty Shells.
MAKES 6 SERVINGS.

Russian Fish and Egg in a Crust

1 package (17-1/4 ounces) frozen Bake It Fresh Puff
   Pastry
2 tablespoons butter or margarine
1 onion, chopped
1/2 cup chopped celery and leaves
1/3 cup flour
1 cup (1/2 pint) light cream
2 cups cooked flaked fish
2 cups cooked rice
4 hard cooked eggs, chopped
1 can (6 ounces) sliced mushrooms, drained
2 eggs, well beaten
Salt and Pepper

Thaw puff pastry 20 minutes, then unfold. In a saucepan, heat butter and sauté onion and celery for 5 minutes. Blend in flour; gradually add light cream and stir over low heat until sauce becomes thick and bubbly. Remove from heat. Fold in fish, rice, hard-cooked eggs, mushrooms and beaten eggs. Season to taste with salt and pepper. Cover and chill.

Place 1 puff pastry sheet on a cookie sheet. Spoon mixture on top of square, spreading mixture to within 1 inch of the edges. Brush edges with water. Roll second sheet to an 11-inch square and place over filling; press edges together. Bake in preheated hot oven (400°) for 40 to 45 minutes or until richly browned. Let stand for 10 minutes, then cut into squares to serve. Can also be served with your favorite sour cream or mushroom sauce.
MAKES 6 TO 8 SERVINGS.

Easy Haddock Mornay

1 pound frozen haddock fillets
Water
1 slice lemon
2 sprigs parsley
1 small onion, peeled
2 peppercorns
1 teaspoon salt
1/2 pound sliced fresh mushrooms
2 tablespoons butter or margarine
1 can (11 ounces) condensed Cheddar cheese soup
1/3 cup milk
1 cup (4 ounces) shredded sharp Cheddar cheese
2 tablespoons dry Sherry
12 slices Honey Wheatberry Bread, crusts trimmed
1/2 cup melted butter or margarine

Place frozen fish in a large saucepan with enough boiling water to cover. Add lemon, parsley, onion, peppercorns, and salt. Simmer covered until the haddock is cooked, about 15 to 20 minutes. Drain and flake haddock.

In a skillet, sauté mushrooms in butter until tender. Stir in soup, milk, and cheese. Fold in haddock and Sherry. Brush both sides of bread slices with melted butter. Press slices into muffin pans. Bake at 350°F for 12 to 15 minutes, or until brown. Spoon haddock mixture into toasted bread cups.
MAKES 6 SERVINGS.

Curried Shrimp

1 package (10 ounces) frozen Bake It Fresh Patty Shells
1/3 cup butter
3 tablespoons flour
1 to 2 tablespoons curry powder
1/2 teaspoon seasoned salt
1/4 teaspoon paprika
2 cups (1 pint) light cream or milk
3 cups shelled and deveined cooked shrimp
1 tablespoon lemon juice
1 teaspoon dry Sherry (optional)
Dash of Worcestershire sauce
2 hard-cooked eggs, chopped
Salt and pepper to taste

Prepare Patty Shells according to package directions. In a saucepan, melt butter; stir in flour, curry powder, seasoned salt, and paprika. Gradually stir in milk or cream; cook, stirring constantly, until mixture thickens. Fold in remaining ingredients and heat through. Season to taste with salt and pepper. Spoon mixture into baked Patty Shells. Serve with sliced orange and red onion salad.
Makes 4 to 6 servings.

Clam Stuffed Trout

4 fresh or frozen trout
Salt and pepper to taste
1/2 cup minced onion
1/2 cup minced celery
1/4 cup butter or margarine
1 can (7-1/2 ounces) minced clams, undrained
1/2 cup clam juice
2 cups Cube Stuffing
1/4 cup melted butter or margarine
Paprika to taste

If trout is fresh, clean and remove head and fin; if trout is frozen, thaw in cold water for 10 minutes. Salt and pepper both inside and out. Sauté onion and celery in butter. Add clams, clam juice, and stuffing; stir over low heat until liquid is absorbed. Stuff trout. Brush top of fish with melted butter; sprinkle with paprika. Bake uncovered at 350°F for 1/2 hour or until fish flakes easily.
Makes 4 servings.

Eggs & Cheese

Creamed Broccoli and Egg Brunch

1 can (10-1/2 ounces) condensed cream of mushroom
    soup
1/3 cup milk
1 cup (4 ounces) shredded Cheddar cheese
1/4 teaspoon dry mustard
Salt and pepper to taste
1 cup cooked broccoli flowerettes
8 slices Canadian bacon
2 tablespoons butter or margarine
2 English Muffins
4 eggs, poached
Dash of nutmeg
Fresh strawberries, if in season

In a saucepan, blend soup and milk until smooth. Cook, stirring until sauce is heated. Stir in cheese and seasonings; heat, stirring until cheese is melted and smooth. Remove 1 cup of this sauce for egg topping; place in small pan and keep warm. Stir broccoli into remaining sauce. Meanwhile, in a skillet, brown bacon in butter. Arrange bacon on toasted English Muffin halves. Top each half with broccoli mixture, then with a poached egg. Cover with cheese sauce and garnish with a dash of nutmeg. Serve with fresh strawberries.
MAKES 4 SERVINGS.

Welsh Rarebit

1 cup beer
2 teaspoons Worcestershire sauce
1 teaspoon dry mustard
4 cups (1 pound) shredded Cheddar cheese
2 eggs, slightly beaten
6 slices of any one of your favorite breads, toasted,
    and cut into quarters
1-1/2 cups chopped fresh tomatoes

In a saucepan, combine beer, Worcestershire sauce, mustard, and cheese. Cook, stirring, until cheese is melted and sauce is smooth. Add several spoonfuls of cheese mixture to beaten eggs and mix well. Return egg mixture to saucepan and cook, stirring, until thickened and smooth. Do not boil. Serve over toast points and garnish with tomato.
MAKES 6 SERVINGS.

Quiche Lorraine

6 slices bacon
1 cup sliced onion, separated into rings
shredded Swiss or Gruyere cheese
1 frozen Deep Dish Pie Shell
3 eggs
1 cup (1/2 pint) heavy cream
1/2 cup milk
1 teaspoon dry mustard
1 teaspoon salt
1/8 teaspoon cayenne pepper

Cook bacon in skillet. Remove, drain, crumble and set aside. Pour off all but 2 tablespoons drippings. Add onion and cook until tender. Place bacon, onions, and cheese in frozen pie shell. Beat together eggs, cream, milk, mustard, salt and pepper. Pour into crust over cheese mixture. Bake in preheated hot oven (450°) for 15 minutes; reduce heat to 325° and bake about 30 to 35 minutes longer or until knife inserted near center comes out clean. Let stand at least 10 minutes before serving. MAKES 6 TO 8 SERVINGS.

Swiss Fondue

1 clove garlic
2 cups dry white wine
3 tablespoons flour
4 cups (1 pound) shredded Swiss or Gruyère cheese
3 tablespoons cherry-flavored brandy or kirsch
1 loaf French Bread, cut into cubes

Rub saucepan or skillet with garlic clove. Add wine and heat until wine is a little bubbly. Mix flour with cheese and gradually add this mixture, one handful at a time, to hot wine. Cook over low heat, stirring after each addition, until cheese is melted and mixture is smooth. Fold in brandy.

Use bread cubes to dip into fondue. Serve fondue in chafing dish or fondue pot. Keep warm during service.
MAKES 6 SERVINGS.

Souffléed Sandwiches

2 tablespoons butter or margarine
6 slices Toasting White Bread, toasted
1/2 pound thinly sliced corned beef
1 pound prepared potato salad
2 tablespoons chopped parsley
2 eggs, separated
1/4 teaspoon salt
2 tablespoons sour cream

Butter toasted bread lightly and place on baking sheet. Top each with corned beef slices. Mix potato salad and parsley. Spoon onto corned beef, flattening out surface.

Beat egg yolk with salt till lemon colored. Fold in sour cream. Beat egg white until stiff but not dry. Fold egg white into egg yolk mixture. Spoon onto potato salad. Bake at 350°F for 12 to 15 minutes or until golden and puffed. Serve with a knife and fork.

MAKES 6 SERVINGS.

Easy Cheese Soufflé

1 teaspoon butter or margarine
3 tablespoons grated Parmesan cheese
3 tablespoons butter or margarine
3 tablespoons flour
1 cup milk
1 teaspoon dry mustard
1/2 teaspoon salt
1/2 teaspoon Worcestershire sauce
1-1/2 cups (6 ounces) shredded Cheddar cheese
6 eggs, separated and at room temperature

Rub a 2-quart soufflé dish with butter and sprinkle with Parmesan cheese. In a saucepan, melt 3 tablespoons butter. Add flour and cook, stirring, 1 minute, or until bubbly and smooth. Remove from heat and gradually stir in milk. Return to heat and cook, stirring until thickened and smooth. Remove from heat and fold in dry mustard, salt, Worcestershire sauce, and cheese, stirring until cheese is melted. Beat in egg yolks one at a time. Beat egg whites until stiff but not dry. Fold egg whites gently into cheese mixture. Spoon into prepared soufflé dish. Bake at 375°F for 35 to 45 minutes, or until golden and puffed and firm to the touch.

MAKES 4 TO 6 SERVINGS.

Garlic Crouton Frittata

1/2 cup sliced mushrooms
1 small clove garlic, minced
3 tablespoons butter or margarine
8 eggs, well beaten
1/4 cup light cream
1 teaspoon salt
1/4 teaspoon oregano
1/8 teaspoon pepper
1/2 cup diced ham
1 cup cubed Mozzarella cheese
2 tablespoons chopped parsley
1-1/2 cups Cheese & Garlic Croutons

In a large oven-proof skillet, brown mushrooms and garlic in butter. Meanwhile, in a bowl, beat together eggs, cream, salt, oregano, and pepper. Pour eggs over mushrooms in skillet. Cook, without stirring, until edges are set. Lift edges of omelet allowing uncooked portions of egg to run underneath. When eggs are brown on bottom, sprinkle with ham, cheese, parlsey, and croutons. Bake at 350°F for 5 minutes, or until cheese is melted and eggs are firm. Serve from skillet, cut into wedges.
MAKES 4 TO 6 SERVINGS.

Eggs Benedict

1/2 cup (1 stick) butter or margarine
3 egg yolks
2 tablespoons lemon juice
1/4 teaspoon salt
Dash of cayenne pepper
6 slices Canadian bacon
3 English Muffins, split and toasted
6 poached eggs

Melt butter in skillet until hot but do not brown. In a blender, combine egg yolks, lemon juice, salt, and pepper. Whirl until smooth. Blend at low speed while gradually dripping in butter. Blend until sauce is smooth and thickened. Keep warm over hot water.

In a skillet, brown bacon. Place bacon on both halves of English Muffins and top each half with a poached egg. Spoon sauce over eggs. Serve immediately.
MAKES 6 SERVINGS.

Garlic Crouton Frittata

Shrimp Egg Fu Yung

1 cup chicken stock or broth
1 tablespoon cornstarch
1 tablespoon soy sauce
1 teaspoon sugar
1 teaspoon cider vinegar
6 eggs, beaten
1 package (6 ounces) frozen, shelled and deveined
    baby shrimp, thawed
1 cup fresh or canned bean sprouts
1/2 cup sliced green onions
1/2 teaspoon salt
1 tablespoon oil

In a saucepan, mix chicken stock and cornstarch until cornstarch is dissolved. Add soy sauce, sugar, and vinegar. Cook, stirring, until sauce is thickened and smooth. Keep warm.

In a bowl, beat eggs. Stir in shrimp, bean sprouts, green onions, and salt. Heat oil in skillet. Make little pancakes by spooning about 3 tablespoons egg mixture for each pancake into skillet. Cook until set; turn and cook until cooked through and lightly browned. Repeat using remaining egg mixture. Serve pancakes topped with sauce.
MAKES 4 TO 6 SERVINGS.

Noodle Pudding

4 cups cooked medium noodles
1 package (1 pound) creamed cottage cheese
1/2 cup golden raisins
1/2 teaspoon salt
1/4 teaspoon ground nutmeg
1 cup (1/2 pint) sour cream
1 cup (1/2 pint) light cream
2 eggs, slightly beaten
2 tablespoons melted butter
1-1/2 cups Sour Cream & Chive Croutons

In a large bowl, combine all ingredients, except croutons. Blend well. Spoon into 2-quart buttered shallow baking dish. Bake at 350°F for 35 minutes. Sprinkle croutons around edge of baking dish. Bake 10 minutes longer, or until pudding is set and golden. Serve warm.
MAKES 6 TO 8 SERVINGS.

Eggs Florentine

1 cup chopped mushrooms
1/4 cup (1/2 stick) butter or margarine
1/4 cup flour
1-1/2 cups milk
1 cup light cream
1 teaspoon salt
1/8 teaspoon pepper
1/4 teaspoon ground nutmeg
3 packages (10 ounces each) frozen chopped spinach,
     cooked and squeezed dry
6 eggs
1/4 cup grated Parmesan cheese
1 cup Onion & Garlic Croutons

In a saucepan, brown mushrooms in butter. Add flour and cook, stirring, until bubbling and smooth. Remove from heat and gradually stir in milk and cream. Cook, stirring, until thickened and smooth. Fold in salt, pepper, nutmeg, and spinach. Spoon into 1-1/2-quart buttered shallow baking dish. Make 6 indentations in spinach and break an egg into each. Sprinkle Parmesan cheese over all. Bake at 325°F for 20 minutes. Sprinkle croutons around edges of casserole and bake 5 to 10 minutes longer, or until eggs are set.
MAKES 6 SERVINGS.

Scrambled Egg Cups

8 slices Honey Bran Bread
6 tablespoons melted butter
8 eggs
1/4 cup milk
Salt and pepper to taste
1 cup shredded, dried beef
2 teaspoons chopped chives or freeze-dried chives

Remove crusts from bread, brush both sides with some of the melted butter; press each bread slice into a large muffin cup. Bake at 350°F for 5 to 10 minutes, or until bread is golden brown. Beat eggs with milk, salt, and pepper until well blended; add dried beef and chives. Heat remaining melted butted in skillet and pour in eggs. Cook over medium heat, stirring frequently. When set, remove from heat and spoon into bread cups.
MAKES 8 SERVINGS.

Eggs in a Hole

Use 1 slice of Toasting White Bread for each serving. Cut a 2-inch diameter hole in the center of each slice using a cookie cutter or an overturned glass.

Heat butter or margarine in a skillet; add bread slices and fry until golden brown on one side. Turn bread and drop an egg into each hole. Sprinkle with salt and pepper. Lower heat and brown slowly until egg white is firm. Fry the round pieces removed from the bread and serve with egg.

Waffled Bread and Cheese

12 slices Family White Bread
6 slices American or Swiss cheese
12 slices cooked bacon
6 tablespoons crunchy peanut butter
2 tablespoons butter or margarine, softened

Make sandwiches using bread, cheese, bacon, and peanut butter. Butter outside of sandwiches. Place on preheated waffle iron. Lower lid and press down gently. Toast sandwiches until golden brown and cheese is melted. Cut into quarters and serve hot.
MAKES 6 SERVINGS.

Eggs Cordon Bleu

1/4 cup melted butter or margarine
1 tablespoon chopped chives
4 French Rolls (6 inches long)
4 slices cooked smoked ham or boiled ham
4 slices cooked chicken or turkey
4 eggs
1/2 cup (2 ounces) shredded sharp Cheddar cheese

In a small bowl, mix butter and chives. With a sharp knife, cut a thin slice from top of rolls. Cut out center of rolls, leaving a shell 1/2-inch thick. (Reserve removed bread for later use in stuffing, bread pudding, or as bread crumbs.) Brush rolls inside and out with butter mixture. Place rolls on a cookie sheet. Line the rolls with slices of ham and turkey. Carefully drop in eggs. Sprinkle top of eggs with cheese. Bake at 350°F for 20 to 25 minutes, or until eggs are set. Serve hot with raw relishes.
MAKES 4 SERVINGS.

Scotch Eggs

1-1/2 pounds ground round
1/4 cup minced onion
2 tablespoons bottled steak sauce
1 teaspoon salt
1/8 teaspoon pepper
2 tablespoons milk
8 hard-cooked eggs, shelled
1 egg, slightly beaten
1 cup Herb Seasoned Stuffing, finely crushed
Oil for frying

In a bowl, combine ground beef, onion, steak sauce, salt, pepper, and milk. Mix well. Shape meat around eggs to cover each egg completely and retain egg shape. Roll each egg in beaten egg and then in stuffing mix.

Fry eggs, 2 to 3 at a time, in preheated deep hot oil (375°F) until golden brown. Turn once. Drain on paper towels. Serve hot.
MAKES 4 SERVINGS.

Goldfish Egg Bake

1 cup chopped celery
1/2 cup chopped green pepper
1/3 cup sliced green onion
1/2 teaspoon salt
1/4 teaspoon dill weed
Generous dash of pepper
1 cup mayonnaise
1/4 cup milk
8 hard-cooked eggs, coarsely chopped
1 cup (4 ounces) shredded Cheddar cheese
1 cup Lightly Salted Goldfish Crackers

In a bowl, combine celery, green pepper, onion, salt, dill, pepper, mayonnaise, and milk; mix well. Stir in eggs just until blended. Place mixture in a 1-quart baking dish and top with cheese. Bake at 350°F for 20 minutes. Sprinkle Goldfish Crackers over casserole and bake 10 minutes longer.
MAKES 4 TO 6 SERVINGS.

French Toast Sandwiches

1 loaf (1 pound) Toasting White Bread
4 eggs
1/4 cup sugar
2 teaspoons vanilla
2 cups milk
1-1/2 teaspoons grated orange peel
1/2 cup butter or margarine
1 cup raspberry or apricot preserves
Confectioners sugar

Separate slices of bread. In shallow bowl, beat eggs, sugar, vanilla, milk, and orange peel until well blended. Dip bread slices into mixture turning to coat both sides. Heat 2 tablespoons of the butter in a large skillet or griddle and brown bread slices on both sides. Add more butter as necessary. Place half the slices on a platter and spread with preserves. Top with remaining slices. Cut sandwiches into halves diagonally and sprinkle with confectioners sugar. Serve warm.
MAKES 6 SERVINGS.

Ham and Rye Casserole

1 cup chopped onion
1/2 cup chopped celery
1/4 cup (1/2 stick) butter or margarine
4 cups cubed Family Rye Bread
1 package (8 ounces) ham, cut into strips
1 package (8 ounces) American cheese, cubed
2-1/2 cups milk
3 eggs
1-1/2 teaspoons prepared mustard
1-1/2 teaspoons salt
1/8 teaspoon pepper

In a saucepan, cook onion and celery in butter until tender. In a 2-quart buttered baking dish, combine sautéed vegetables with bread, ham, and half the cheese.

In a bowl, beat together milk, eggs, mustard, salt, and pepper until well blended. Pour over ingredients in casserole and top with remaining cheese. Bake at 350°F for 1 hour, or until golden brown and puffed.
MAKES 4 TO 6 SERVINGS.

Vegetables

Pickled Artichoke and Hearts of Palm

2 cans (8 ounces each) artichoke hearts, well drained
1 can (14 ounces) hearts of palm, well drained
2 tablespoons chopped scallions
2 tablespoons chopped pimiento
1 tablespoon chopped chives
1 tablespoon finely chopped parsley

6 tablespoons olive or vegetable oil
2 tablespoons red wine or apple cider vinegar
1 clove garlic, minced
Salt and pepper to taste

Watercress
Sprouted Wheat Bread

Slice artichoke hearts in half; slice hearts of palm into 1/2-inch pieces. Mix together with scallions, pimiento, chives, and parsley.

In a small bowl, mix oil, wine, garlic, and salt and pepper to taste. Pour this dressing over artichokes and hearts of palm. Cover and let stand at least 1 hour. Mix well and serve on a bed of watercress with slices of bread.

MAKES 4 SERVINGS.

Peas Epicurean

6 slices bacon, chopped
1 small onion, chopped
1/2 pound mushrooms, chopped
1 tablespoon flour
1 cup milk
1/4 cup heavy cream
2 packages (10 ounces each) frozen peas
Salt and pepper to taste

Cook bacon in skillet until crisp. Remove, drain, and crumble; set aside. Pour off all but 2 tablespoons of drippings. Add onion and mushrooms and cook until golden. Reduce heat; stir in flour. Remove from heat and gradually blend in milk, cream, peas, and salt and pepper to taste. Cook, stirring constantly, until mixture thickens. Serve sprinkled with crumbled bacon.

MAKES 6 SERVINGS.

Red Cabbage and Apples

1 small head red cabbage, cored
2 tart apples
1 tablespoon butter or margarine
1 medium onion, peeled and chopped
1/4 cup cider vinegar
3 tablespoons red currant jelly
1/4 cup water
1/4 teaspoon salt
Pinch of pepper

Shred cabbage; peel, core, and grate apples. Melt butter in a saucepan, add onion and sauté for 2 minutes. Mix in cabbage, apples, cider vinegar, jelly, water, salt, and pepper. Cover and simmer 45 minutes to 1 hour, or until cabbage is tender, stirring occasionally. Serve hot or cold.
MAKES 6 SERVINGS.

Sunday Night Casserole

2-1/2 cups Herb Seasoned Stuffing
1 package (10 ounces) frozen broccoli spears, thawed
    and drained
6 hard-cooked eggs, quartered
2 cans (10-3/4 ounces each) condensed cream of
    chicken soup
2/3 cup milk
1 teaspoon instant minced onion
1/8 teaspoon instant minced garlic
1 cup (4 ounces) shredded Cheddar cheese
1/4 cup grated Parmesan cheese
3/4 teaspoon dry mustard
1/4 cup (1/2 stick) butter or margarine, melted
1/4 cup hot water

Sprinkle 1 cup of the stuffing into buttered 9-inch shallow baking dish. Arrange broccoli and eggs on top of stuffing.

In a saucepan, mix soup with milk until smooth. Add onion and garlic; heat, stirring until smooth. Pour over broccoli and egg mixture. Mix remaining stuffing with cheeses, dry mustard, butter, and water. Spoon over casserole. Bake at 400°F for 30 minutes, or until lightly browned and bubbling.
MAKES 4 TO 6 SERVINGS.

Eggplant Parmesan

2 medium eggplants
1/4 cup flour
Vegetable oil for frying
3/4 cup cottage cheese
1/2 cup Ricotta cheese
2 cans (8 ounces each) tomato sauce
1 teaspoon oregano
1 cloved garlic, minced
Salt and pepper to taste
1/2 cup (2 ounces) grated Mozzarella cheese
1/2 cup grated Parmesan cheese

Peel and slice eggplants into 6 to 8 slices each. Dip slices into flour and sauté in shallow oil on both sides until golden brown. Drain on paper towels. In a small bowl, mix cottage and Ricotta cheeses together. In another bowl, mix tomato sauce, oregano, minced garlic, and salt and pepper to taste.

In a baking dish, layer in order: half the eggplant, half the tomato sauce mixture, and half the cheese mixture. Repeat. Top with grated Mozzarella, then Parmesan cheese. Bake uncovered at 350°F for 30 to 40 minutes.

Makes 6 servings.

Scalloped Potatoes With Sour Cream and Chive Topping

Butter or margarine
1 clove garlic, peeled
3 pounds potatoes, peeled, and very thinly sliced
1 cup (1/2 pint) half-and-half
Ground nutmeg to taste
Salt and pepper to taste
3/4 cup (3 ounces) Gruyère cheese, grated
1/2 cup Sour Cream & Chive Croutons
Parsley for garnish

Butter the bottom and sides of a 1-1/2-quart casserole, then rub with garlic. Arrange potatoes in layers in the dish. Heat half-and-half in a saucepan and add nutmeg, salt, and pepper to taste. Pour this mixture over potatoes. Sprinkle cheese and croutons over potato mixture. Dot with butter and bake at 350°F for 40 to 50 minutes, or until potatoes are tender. Serve sprinkled with chopped parsley.

Makes 6 to 8 servings.

Orange Sweet Potato Pie

2 medium-sized sweet potatoes, boiled in their skins
   until fork tender
1/2 cup sugar
1/4 cup firmly packed light brown sugar
1/2 teaspoon salt
1/8 teaspoon nutmeg
2 eggs, beaten
1 teaspoon vanilla
1/4 cup butter
1 cup (1/2 pint) half and half
1 orange
1 frozen Deep Dish Pie Shell

Remove skins from sweet potatoes and mash. Add sugars, salt, nutmeg, eggs and vanilla. Melt butter in a saucepan with half and half. Grate the rind of the orange and add to the milk mixture. Peel the orange and cut into slices; place on bottom of frozen pastry shell. Fold the milk mixture into the sweet potato mixture. Pour into pastry shell and bake in preheated hot oven (450°) for 10 minutes. Reduce heat to 350° and bake 45 minutes longer or until a knife inserted in center comes out clean. Serve warm.

MAKES 6 TO 8 SERVINGS.

Cheesey Potato Pancakes

3 medium-sized potatoes, peeled and shredded
1 medium onion, peeled, finely chopped
2 eggs, beaten
2/3 cup crushed Cheddar & Romano Croutons
Salt and pepper to taste
Vegetable oil for shallow pan frying
Applesauce

Shred potatoes into a bowl of cold water. This keeps them from turning brown and removes excess starch. Drain.

In a bowl, mix together potatoes and onion. Fold in eggs, croutons, and salt and pepper to taste. Heat oil, about 1/4-inch deep, in skillet and drop potato mixture by spoonfuls into the oil. Fry pancakes until golden on one side, then turn and fry on the other side. Drain on paper towels. Serve warm with applesauce.

MAKES 4 TO 6 SERVINGS.

Broccoli With Tuna Sauce

2 bunches fresh broccoli
Water
1 tablespoon butter or margarine
1 small onion, grated
2 tablespoons flour
2 cups milk
2 cans (6 ounces each) tuna, drained and flaked
Juice of 1/2 lemon
Salt and pepper to taste
1/2 cup (2 ounces) grated Cheddar cheese
1/2 cup Sour Cream & Chive Croutons

Clean broccoli and place in a saucepan with about 1 inch of boiling water. Cover; simmer until tender (about 10 minutes). Drain and arrange pieces in a well-buttered 2-quart casserole.

Meanwhile, melt butter in a saucepan, add grated onion and sauté for 3 minutes. Add flour and cook several minutes, stirring, until bubbling and smooth. Remove from heat and gradually stir in milk. Return to heat. Cook, stirring constantly until sauce is thickened and smooth. Fold in tuna and lemon juice and simmer 1 minute more. Season to taste with salt and pepper. Pour sauce over broccoli. Combine grated cheese and croutons and spread over top of casserole. Place casserole under broiler for a few minutes until cheese melts. Serve immediately.
MAKES 6 TO 8 SERVINGS.

Crusty Carrot Sticks

6 fresh carrots, scraped
1 egg, beaten
1/4 cup milk
1 cup Cheddar & Romano Croutons

Cut carrots into quarters lengthwise, then in half crosswise. Combine the egg and milk in a shallow bowl. Crush croutons to fine crumbs with a rolling pin, blender, or food processor. Dip the carrot sticks first into the egg mixture, then into the crouton crumbs. Arrange on an oiled cookie sheet and bake at 375°F for 30 minutes, turning carrots once or twice during the baking time.
MAKES 4 TO 6 SERVINGS.

Fruity Walnut Stuffed Peppers

1 can (8 ounces) unsweetened sliced peaches or
    pineapple chunks
3 large red and 3 large green peppers
Water
1 teaspoon salt
2 medium onions, diced
2 tablespoons butter or margarine
3 cups Herb Seasoned Stuffing
1/2 cup chopped walnuts
1 cup (4 ounces) grated Cheddar cheese
2 eggs, beaten
Salt and pepper to taste

Drain fruit, reserving juice. Dice fruit and set aside. Cut off tops of peppers and remove seeds. Place peppers and tops in enough boiling, salted water to cover. Reduce heat and simmer 8 minutes. Invert and drain on paper towels.

Meanwhile, in a saucepan, sauté onions in butter until golden. Remove from heat and mix in reserved fruit, juice, and remaining ingredients. Fill peppers with stuffing mixture, replace tops and place in a shallow casserole with 1/2 inch of water on the bottom. Bake at 350°F for 25 to 30 minutes. Serve hot.

MAKES 6 SERVINGS.

Celery Waldorf

1 bunch celery
2 cups chicken stock or consommé
1 green cooking apple, peeled and sliced
2 tablespoons butter or margarine
1/2 cup walnuts
1 cup Herb Seasoned Stuffing
1 teaspoon sugar
1/2 cup water
Salt and pepper to taste

Cut celery into 2-inch pieces. Combine celery and chicken stock in baking dish and set aside.

Briefly sauté apple slices in butter. Stir in walnuts, stuffing, sugar, water, and salt and pepper to taste. Pour this mixture over celery and bake at 400°F for 20 to 30 minutes.

MAKES 4 TO 6 SERVINGS.

y Walnut Stuffed Peppers

Cauliflower Casserole

1 medium head cauliflower
Water
3 tablespoons butter or margarine
1/4 cup flour
2 cups milk
3/4 teaspoon salt
1/8 teaspoon pepper
1 package (8 ounces) Herb Seasoned Stuffing
1 cup water
1/2 cup melted butter or margarine

Break cauliflower into small pieces and place in a saucepan with about 1 inch of boiling water. Cover and simmer until tender (about 10 minutes). Drain and place in a shallow 2-quart casserole.

Melt butter in a medium saucepan. Stir in flour and cook together for a few minutes, stirring constantly. Remove from heat and blend in milk, salt, and pepper. Bring to a boil, stirring constantly and simmer until thickened. Pour sauce over cauliflower in casserole. Mix stuffing, water, and melted butter, and spread evenly on top of ingredients in casserole. Bake at 350°F for 30 minutes.
MAKES 8 TO 10 SERVINGS.

Note: Broccoli may be used in place of cauliflower.

Cabbage With Orange and Raisins

1 orange, juiced
1/2 cup raisins
1/2 head green cabbage, shredded
1 onion, chopped
1 teaspoon salt
1/8 teaspoon pepper
1/2 teaspoon caraway seeds

In a small bowl, combine orange juice and raisins. Leave them to soak for 1 hour. Place 1 inch of water in the bottom of a large saucepan and bring to a boil; add cabbage and onion and cook covered over low heat for 10 to 12 minutes, or until cabbage is tender. Fold in raisins, orange juice, salt, pepper, and caraway seeds. Cook uncovered 3 minutes more.
MAKES 4 TO 6 SERVINGS.

Irene's Corn Pudding

4 eggs
1 cup milk
2 cans (17 ounces each) creamed corn
1/2 teaspoon salt
2 tablespoons flour
1 tablespoon sugar
Butter or margarine

In a large bowl, beat eggs and milk together. Fold in corn, salt, flour, and sugar. Grease a 1-1/2-quart casserole with butter or margarine and pour mixture into casserole. Bake at 350°F for 1 to 1-1/4 hours, or until the top browns. Serve immediately.
MAKES 8 TO 10 SERVINGS.

Carrot and Nut Loaf

2 cups grated carrots
2 cups Herb Seasoned Stuffing
1/2 cup grated Cheddar cheese
1 large onion, finely grated
1/2 cup chopped nuts
3 eggs, lightly beaten
1 cup half-and-half
Parsley for garnish

In a large bowl, combine grated carrots, stuffing, cheese, onion, and nuts. In a separate bowl beat eggs with half-and-half. Fold egg mixture into the carrot mixture and pour into a buttered 9 x 5 x 3-inch loaf pan. Bake at 350°F for 1 hour, or until knife inserted in the middle comes out clean. Garnish with chopped parsley.
MAKES 4 TO 6 SERVINGS.

Herb Crusted Vegetables

2 large Bermuda onions, peeled
2 potatoes, peeled
2 zucchini
1 egg, beaten
1/4 cup milk
1 cup Herb Seasoned Stuffing
Oil

Cut onions and potatoes in 1/4-inch slices and zucchini into 1/2-inch slices. Beat egg and milk in a shallow bowl. Crush stuffing to fine crumbs with a rolling pin, blender, or food processor. Dip vegetable slices, first into the egg mixture, then into the stuffing. Arrange vegetables in a single layer on an oiled cookie sheet and bake at 375°F for 30 to 40 minutes, or until vegetables are tender, brown, and crisp.
MAKES 4 TO 6 SERVINGS.

Herbed Asparagus

2 packages (10 ounces each) frozen asparagus, thawed
1 cup water
1/2 onion, chopped
2 tablespoons oil
1/2 green pepper, diced
1/2 red pepper, diced
1 cup Herb Seasoned Stuffing
1 hard-cooked egg, finely chopped

In a buttered baking dish, arrange asparagus in a single layer. Pour 1/2 cup of the water over asparagus. In a skillet, sauté onion in oil for 3 minutes; add green and red pepper, cook 2 minutes longer. Remove from heat and fold in stuffing and remaining water. Mix thoroughly and spread evenly over asparagus. Bake at 350°F for 15 to 20 minutes, or until topping is crispy. Garnish with hard-cooked egg.
MAKES 4 TO 6 SERVINGS.

German Potatoes With Scallions and Celery

3 pounds new potatoes
3 stalks celery, chopped
1/2 cup coarsely chopped parsley
2 tablespoons butter or margarine
1/2 cup chopped scallions
1/4 cup finely chopped parsley
1/2 cup Onion & Garlic Croutons
Salt and pepper to taste

Cook potatoes, celery, and chopped parsley in enough boiling water to cover, until potatoes are tender. Drain. Fold in butter, scallions, parsley, and croutons. Season to taste with salt and pepper. Serve immediately.
MAKES 4 TO 6 SERVINGS.

Chinese Stir-Fried Vegetables

1 medium onion, finely chopped
1/4 pound mushrooms
1/2 green pepper, sliced
1/2 red pepper, sliced
1/4 pound bean sprouts
2 tablespoons soy sauce
1/2 teaspoon salt
1/4 teaspoon sugar
Pinch of pepper
3/4 cup chicken broth or chicken consommé
1-1/2 tablespoons cornstarch
3 tablespoons vegetable oil
1 clove garlic, minced
1 slice fresh peeled ginger root
1 tablespoon Sherry wine
2 scallions, diced
Soft Family Rolls

Prepare all vegetables ahead and set aside. In a bowl, combine soy sauce, salt, sugar, pepper, and 1/2 cup chicken stock. Mix remaining 1/4 cup stock with cornstarch and set aside.

Heat oil in a wok or heavy skillet. Add garlic and ginger root; stir quickly; add onion and stir fry for 1 minute. Add mushrooms, green and red pepper; fry for another minute then add bean sprouts, cook for 30 seconds more. Stir in the soy sauce mixture and thicken with cornstarch mixture. Bring to a boil, stir in Sherry. Sprinkle with scallions and serve immediately with warmed rolls.

MAKES 4 SERVINGS.

Chinese Stir-Fried Broccoli and Cashew Nuts

3 tablespoons vegetable oil
1 onion, diced
2 stalks celery, cut into 1-inch pieces
1 bunch fresh broccoli, cleaned and broken into
    flowerettes
1/2 red pepper, cut into 1/4-inch strips
1 teaspoon salt
2 tablespoons soy sauce
1/2 cup cashew nuts
2 scallions, diced

Heat oil in a wok or heavy skillet. Stir fry onion for 3 minutes; add celery and broccoli and continue stir frying until vegetables are a bright green color. Add red pepper and stir fry another 2 minutes. Stir in salt, soy sauce, nuts, and scallions. Serve immediately.
MAKES 4 TO 6 SERVINGS.

Green Beans Italienne

1 tablespoon oil
1 medium-sized onion, chopped
2 tomatoes, peeled and chopped
1/2 green pepper, diced
1/2 cup water
1 clove garlic, crushed
1 bay leaf
1 teaspoon salt
1 pound green beans, fresh or frozen, cut into 1-inch
  pieces
1/2 cup Onion & Garlic Croutons

Heat oil in a saucepan, add onions, and sauté for 3 minutes. Add tomatoes, pepper, water, garlic, bay leaf, and salt. Simmer, covered for 10 minutes; stirring occasionally. Add beans, cover and simmer another 10 to 15 minutes, or until beans are cooked. Remove bay leaf. Sprinkle croutons on top and serve.
MAKES 4 TO 6 SERVINGS.

Yellow and Green Beans Meuniere

1 pound fresh wax beans
1/2 pound fresh green beans
2 tablespoons light cream (optional)
2 tablespoons chopped parsley
Salt and pepper to taste
1/2 cup Onion & Garlic Croutons

Trim and cut beans into 2-inch lengths. Place in saucepan with 1 inch of boiling water. Cover and simmer 10 to 15 minutes; drain. Add cream, parsley, and salt and pepper to taste. Simmer for 2 to 3 minutes, or until beans are tender. Serve hot sprinkled with croutons.
MAKES 6 SERVINGS.

Salads

Molded Melon Salad With Yogurt Dressing

2 envelopes unflavored gelatin
1/3 cup sugar
1/4 cup water
3 cups lemon lime soda
1/2 cup orange liqueur
4 cups diced, peeled, and seeded cantaloupe
2 cups stemmed seedless grapes
1 cup lemon yogurt
1/4 cup orange juice
Strawberry halves for garnish
1 head Iceberg lettuce, cored, and separated into leaves
Butter Crescent Rolls

In a small saucepan, combine gelatin, sugar, and water. Stir over low heat until sugar and gelatin are dissolved. Pour mixture into a bowl and stir in soda and liqueur. Stir well and chill until slightly thickened. Fold in cantaloupe and grapes and pour into a 1-1/2-quart mold. Chill until firm. In a small bowl, mix yogurt and orange juice. Chill. When ready to serve, dip mold into lukewarm water for a few seconds. Loosen edges with the tip of a knife, tap to loosen, and invert onto a platter. Garnish with strawberry halves. Serve spooned into lettuce cups with yogurt sauce spooned over each serving. Serve with rolls.
MAKES 6 SERVINGS.

Pineapple Salad

1 can (1 pound, 4 ounces) pineapple chunks, drained
1/2 pound fresh or 1 can (1 pound) bean sprouts, drained
1/2 cup chopped celery
1/2 cup oil
1/2 cup orange juice
1/2 teaspoon salt
2 tablespoons toasted sesame seeds
1-1/2 cups croutons, any flavor
2 cups shredded lettuce

In a bowl, combine pineapple, bean sprouts, and celery. In a small bowl, beat oil, orange juice, and salt until thick. Stir in sesame seeds. Pour dressing over pineapple mixture and toss. Chill. When ready to serve, stir in croutons. Line serving plates with lettuce and top with pineapple mixture.
MAKES 6 SERVINGS.

Salade Niçoise

3 hard-cooked eggs, quartered
1 can (7 ounces) tuna, drained and flaked
2 medium tomatoes, cut in wedges
1/2 cup sliced black olives
1/2 cup sliced stuffed olives
1 can (2 ounces) anchovies
2 tablespoons capers

1/2 cup olive oil
2 tablespoons wine vinegar
1/2 teaspoon dry mustard
1 clove garlic
1/4 teaspoon basil

1 head Boston lettuce, cored and separated into leaves
1-1/2 cups Cheese & Garlic Croutons

In a large bowl, combine eggs, tuna, tomatoes, olives, anchovies, and capers.

In a small bowl, beat oil, vinegar, mustard, garlic, and basil until thick. Just before serving, pour dressing over tuna mixture and toss well. Arrange on lettuce leaves and top with croutons.

MAKES 4 SERVINGS.

Dutch Wilted Lettuce Salad

4 strips bacon, diced
2 teaspoons firmly-packed brown sugar
2 scallions, sliced
1/2 teaspoon salt
2 tablespoons cider vinegar
1/4 teaspoon dry mustard
Dash of paprika
1 head Iceberg lettuce, cored and shredded
1-1/2 cups croutons, any flavor

In a skillet, fry bacon until crisp and add remaining ingredients except lettuce and croutons. Bring to a boil. In a salad bowl, tear lettuce into bite-size pieces. Toss with hot bacon mixture. Serve warm sprinkled with croutons.

MAKES 6 SERVINGS.

Bean Salad

1 package (9 ounces) frozen cut green beans
1 package (9 ounces) frozen cut wax beans
1 can (1 pound) kidney beans, drained
1 cup cooked chick peas or drained canned chick peas
1 small red onion, thinly sliced
1/2 cup thinly sliced green pepper
1/3 cup salad oil
3 tablespoons cider vinegar
1/2 teaspoon dry mustard
1 small clove garlic, minced
1/2 teaspoon celery seed
2 cups Onion & Garlic Croutons
Crisp greens

Cook beans in lightly salted water until tender. Drain. Combine with remaining ingredients except croutons and greens. Toss well to blend. Chill until ready to serve. Toss salad with croutons; spoon mixture onto a bed of greens.
MAKES 6 SERVINGS.

Cauliflower Combo

2 cups raw cauliflowerettes
1 cup sliced raw mushrooms
1/3 cup sliced radishes
1 cup halved cherry tomatoes
1/2 cup green pepper strips
1/4 cup chopped red peppers
3 tablespoons sliced green onions
1/2 cup oil
3 tablespoons wine vinegar
1/4 teaspoon dry mustard
1 small clove garlic, mashed
1/2 teaspoon salt
1 cup Taco Goldfish Crackers
Salad greens

In a bowl, combine all ingredients except crackers and greens. Toss to blend well. Chill at least 3 hours. Toss several times during chilling. To serve, fold in Goldfish Crackers. Spoon onto greens.
MAKES 6 SERVINGS.

Caesar Salad à la Pepperidge

1 cup Onion & Garlic Croutons
1-1/2 tablespoons anchovy paste
1 tablespoon olive oil
2 medium heads Romaine lettuce
1/8 teaspoon salt
Freshly ground pepper to taste
1/4 cup olive oil
1/3 cup freshly grated Parmesan cheese
1 egg
1 teaspoon Worcestershire sauce
2 tablespoons lime juice

Toss croutons in anchovy paste mixed with olive oil until croutons are lightly coated.

Core, wash, dry, and chill lettuce. Tear into bite-size pieces, removing heavy ribs. Place greens in large wooden bowl. Sprinkle with salt and pepper. Dribble oil over leaves and toss until evenly coated. Sprinkle on cheese. Add prepared croutons. Cook egg in boiling water 50 seconds only and break over salad. Add Worcestershire and lime juice. Toss in bowl until well mixed with all greens, and well coated with dressing. Serve immediately.

MAKES 4 TO 6 SERVINGS.

Turkey Rice Salad

3 cups diced cooked turkey
3 cups cold cooked white or brown rice
1/2 cup sliced stuffed olives
1/2 cup raisins or currants
1/2 cup olive oil
1/3 cup red wine vinegar
1 tablespoon sugar
1/4 teaspoon garlic powder
1/2 teaspoon curry powder
Tomato slices
French Bread

Combine all ingredients except tomato slices and French Bread in a large bowl and stir until well blended. Pour into a salad bowl and surround with tomato slices. Chill for several hours. Serve with slices of French Bread.

MAKES 6 SERVINGS.

Taco Ensalada

8 small cooked beets
4 oranges, peeled (white membrane removed)
4 red apples, unpeeled but cored
4 bananas, peeled
1 fresh pineapple, peeled and cored or 1 can (1 pound,
    4 ounces) pineapple chunks, drained
1/4 cup sugar (optional)
1 head Iceberg lettuce, cored and separated into leaves

1/2 cup oil
3/4 cup orange juice
1-1/2 tablespoons sugar
Juice of 1 lime

1 package Taco Goldfish Crackers

Thinly slice the beets, oranges, apples, bananas, and pineapple (if fresh). Combine beets and fruits in a large shallow bowl and sprinkle with the sugar, if you choose to use it. To serve, spoon portions of salad on a bed of lettuce and chill.

In a small bowl, beat oil, orange juice, sugar, and lime juice until sugar is dissolved. Just before serving, pour dressing over salad; garnish with Goldfish Crackers.

MAKES 6 TO 8 SERVINGS.

Fruited Tuna Salad

2 cans (6-1/2 ounces each) chunk-style tuna, drained
2 cups sliced celery
2 cups halved seedless green grapes
1 can (11 ounces) mandarin oranges, drained
2 tablespoons chopped scallions
1 cup mayonnaise
1 tablespoon lemon juice
1 head Boston lettuce, cored, and separated into leaves
Lightly Salted Goldfish Crackers

In a bowl, mix tuna, celery, grapes, oranges, and scallions. Stir in mayonnaise and lemon juice. Chill. When ready to serve, line a salad bowl with lettuce leaves. Spoon on salad and sprinkle each serving with Goldfish Crackers.

MAKES 6 SERVINGS.

*Fruited Tuna Salad
and Taco Ensalada*

Avocado Orange Salad With Frozen Horseradish Cream

2 cups (1 pint) heavy cream
1/4 cup white horseradish
2 teaspoons prepared yellow mustard
1/2 teaspoon salt
1/2 teaspoon pepper

3 avocados
3 oranges
Lettuce leaves
Parker House Rolls

Make horseradish cream the day or morning before serving salad. In a large bowl, beat heavy cream until thick. Fold in horseradish, mustard, salt and pepper. Line bottom and sides of a 9-inch square pan with foil. Pour in horseradish mixture; freeze several hours, or until hard. Use foil to lift cream out of pan and cut into 1-inch cubes while still frozen.

Peel avocados, cut in half, remove seed. Peel and cut oranges into sections. Arrange a few orange sections in the center of each avocado. Serve on a bed of lettuce with several cubes of frozen horseradish cream. Serve with rolls.

MAKES 6 SERVINGS.

Make Your Own Salad Bar Buffet at Home

SALAD INGREDIENTS: ARRANGE IN SEPARATE BOWLS
Several varieties of salad greens, trimmed, washed, and
    torn into bite-size pieces
Spinach leaves, washed and trimmed
Raw broccoli and cauliflower flowerets
Shredded raw carrots
Sliced red onions and radishes
Tomato wedges
Strips of raw green pepper
Kidney beans or chick peas
Shredded cheese or crumbled blue cheese
Diced beef, chicken, turkey, or ham
Cottage cheese
Shrimp, tuna, salmon, sardines, or crabmeat
Hard-cooked eggs
Croutons, Goldfish and Snack Sticks, all flavors

SALAD DRESSINGS: SEVERAL KINDS IN BOWLS OR CRUETS

Let everyone make their own combination. Add plenty of assorted breads and rolls and coffee to drink. Serve a few cookies and pieces of cake to complete an easy, not too caloric, meal.

Creamy Blue Cheese Dressing: Combine 3 ounces blue or Roquefort cheese, 1-1/2 cups olive or corn oil, 2 cloves garlic, crushed, 1/4 cup cider vinegar, and 3 tablespoons sugar in a blender and whirl until smooth. Season to taste with salt and pepper. Chill.
MAKES 2 CUPS.

Honey Lime Dressing: Combine 1/3 cup lime juice, 3 tablespoons honey, and 1 cup corn oil in a blender and whirl until smooth. Season to taste with salt. Chill and beat again before serving.
MAKES 1-1/2 CUPS.

Low Calorie Creamy Dressing: Place 1 cup (8 ounces) low-fat or skim milk cottage cheese, 1/4 teaspoon garlic powder, 1 teaspoon paprika, 1 cup plain yogurt, and salt to taste in a blender and whirl until smooth. Chill.
MAKES 2 CUPS.

Low Calorie Tomato Dressing: In a bowl, combine 1 cup tomato juice, 1 envelope dehydrated chicken broth (1 serving), 1 tablespoon grated onion, 1 teaspoon Worcestershire sauce, and 1/4 cup lemon juice and stir until well blended. Chill.
MAKES 1-1/2 CUPS.

Orange Pico Salad

2 navel oranges, peeled, sliced, and seeded
1 cucumber, sliced
1 head Romaine lettuce, cored, and torn into bite-size
    pieces
1 small onion, sliced, separated into rings

1/2 cup corn oil
1/4 cup orange juice
2 tablespoons cider vinegar
1-1/2 teaspoons sugar
Salt and pepper to taste

1-1/2 cups Croutons, any flavor

In a salad bowl, mix together first 4 ingredients. In a small bowl, beat oil, orange juice, cider vinegar, sugar, salt and pepper until thick. Just before serving, pour dressing over salad and toss lightly. Sprinkle with croutons. MAKES 6 SERVINGS.

Spinach Salad

1 pound fresh spinach
2 medium oranges, peeled and sliced
1 medium red onion, thinly sliced (about 1 cup)
1/3 cup cooked and crumbled bacon

1/2 cup mayonnaise
1/2 cup olive oil
1/4 cup lemon juice
2 teaspoons prepared mustard

1 cup Parmesan Cheese Goldfish Crackers

Wash spinach thoroughly, remove stems and tear leaves into bite-size pieces. In a salad bowl, mix spinach, oranges, onion, and bacon.

In a small bowl, mix mayonnaise, oil, lemon juice, and mustard. Just before serving, pour dressing over salad and toss lightly. Garnish with Goldfish Crackers.
MAKES 4 TO 6 SERVINGS.

Perfection Salad

1 envelope unflavored gelatin
1/4 cup sugar
1/2 teaspoon salt
1-1/4 cups water
1/4 cup cider vinegar
1 tablespoon lemon juice
1/2 cup finely shredded green cabbage
1 cup chopped celery
1/2 apple, peeled and thinly sliced
Additional shredded green cabbage for garnish
1/4 cup mayonnaise
1/4 cup sour cream
Wheat Germ Bread

Mix gelatin, sugar, and salt in a small saucepan. Stir in 1/2 cup of the water. Place over low heat, stirring constantly until gelatin is dissolved. Remove from heat and stir in remaining water, cider vinegar, and lemon juice. Chill until slightly thickened. Fold in cabbage, celery, and apple. Pour into a 4-cup mold and chill until firm. To unmold, dip into lukewarm water for a few seconds, tap to loosen, and invert onto a platter. Surround with additional shredded cabbage. Serve with mayonnaise mixed with sour cream and bread and butter sandwiches made with bread.
MAKES 4 SERVINGS.

Salmon Mousse With Cucumber Dressing

MOUSSE
2 envelopes unflavored gelatin
2 cups chicken broth
Juice of 1 lemon
1 can (7 ounces) salmon, drained, skinned, and boned
1/2 cup finely chopped celery
1/2 cup chopped ripe olives
1 cup (1/2 pint) sour cream
Salt to taste

DRESSING
1 cup mayonnaise
1/4 cup lemon juice
1/2 cup peeled, seeded, and shredded cucumber
1/4 cup capers
1/4 teaspoon fines herbes

1 head lettuce, cored and separated into leaves
Sesame Seed Buns

In a small saucepan, mix gelatin and 1/2 cup of the chicken broth; stir over low heat until gelatin is dissolved. Pour mixture into a bowl and stir in remaining chicken broth and lemon juice. Chill until slightly thickened. Fold in salmon, celery, olives, and sour cream. Season to taste with salt. Pour mixture into a lightly-oiled, 5-cup mold or fish mold. Chill until firm.

In a small bowl combine all dressing ingredients and mix until well blended. Chill. When ready to serve, dip mold into lukewarm water for a few seconds, tap to loosen, and invert onto a lettuce leaf-lined serving platter. Serve with dressing and warmed Sesame Seed Buns.
MAKES 6 SERVINGS.

Hot Meat and Potato Salad

4 cups diced cooked potatoes
2 cups diced cooked beef or other meat
1 bunch scallions, trimmed and sliced
2 large carrots, shredded
1 cup sliced celery
1 cup mayonnaise
3 tablespoons prepared yellow mustard
3 tablespoons white horseradish
Salt and pepper to taste
Lettuce leaves
Radishes for garnish
Family Rye Bread

Combine all ingredients except radishes and bread in a large bowl and toss until well blended. Season to taste with salt and pepper. Chill covered for several hours. Spoon mixture into a bowl lined with lettuce leaves. Decorate with radish slices and serve with slices of bread.
MAKES 6 SERVINGS.

Cottage Cheese Luncheon Salad

2 cups (1 pound) cottage cheese
1 cup sliced radishes
1 raw carrot, shredded
1 tablespoon chopped green onion
Lettuce leaves
2 green peppers, seeded, and cut into rings
3 tomatoes, sliced
6 scallions, sliced
1/2 cup low-calorie Italian salad dressing
Very Thin White or Rye Bread
Celery or onion salt to taste

In a bowl, mix cottage cheese with radishes, carrots, and green onion. Line salad plates with lettuce leaves. Spoon cottage cheese mixture on lettuce and garnish with green peppers, tomatoes, and scallions. Chill. Serve topped with salad dressing. Serve with slices of toasted bread, sprinkled with celery or onion salt.
MAKES 6 SERVINGS.

Sandwiches

Hangtown Fry in a Roll

1/4 cup butter or margarine
1 onion, chopped
1/2 cup chopped celery
1/3 cup chopped parsley
6 eggs
6 tablespoons milk
1 teaspoon salt
1/4 teaspoon pepper
2 cans (8 ounces each) oysters, drained
1 package (12 ounces) French Rolls
2 tomatoes, cut into slices

In a large skillet, melt butter or margarine. Sauté onion, celery, and parsley for about 5 minutes, or until lightly browned. Beat eggs with milk, salt, and pepper, and add to skillet. Add oysters and stir gently until eggs are moist but firm. Split rolls in half lengthwise. Pile hot egg mixture on bottom of rolls; top with tomato slices and tops of rolls. Serve hot. MAKES 4 SERVINGS.

NOTE: 1 cup diced cooked chicken, ham, shrimp, crabmeat, or tuna may be used instead of oysters. Can also be made with 1/2-cup canned smoked oysters, or pieces of smoked salmon.

Super-Duper Sandwich

12 slices Honey Wheatberry Bread
1 can (1 pound, 4 ounces) chick peas, drained
1/4 cup prepared Italian salad dressing
2 hard-cooked eggs, sieved
1 cup shredded lettuce
1/3 cup shredded carrots
1/3 cup shredded zucchini
1 red pepper, chopped
12 slices crisp cooked bacon
2 tablespoons toasted sesame seeds

Toast bread. If desired, remove hulls from chick peas. Mash chick peas and beat in salad dressing and eggs. Spread mixture on 6 of the bread slices. Top with lettuce, carrots, zucchini, red pepper, bacon slices, and sesame seeds. Cover with remaining bread slices. MAKES 6 SERVINGS.

Sandwiches By The Inch

1 loaf (16 ounces) Family Rye Bread
1 package (8 ounces) cream cheese
2 tablespoons chopped chives
1/4 cup milk
1 package (8 ounces) sharp Cheddar cheese
1 clove garlic, mashed
2 teaspoons Worcestershire sauce
Dry Sherry

Unwrap bread slices and place them all side by side on a table. Remove 1 slice and reserve. In a bowl, mix cream cheese, chives, and milk until light and fluffy. In another bowl, grate Cheddar cheese finely and stir in garlic, Worcestershire sauce, and enough Sherry to make a spreadable consistency. Spread half of the slices with cream cheese mixture and half with the Sherry-cheese mixture. Reshape the loaf of bread, alternating cream cheese-spread slices with Cheddar cheese-spread slices and ending with the plain slice of bread. Chill for several hours. With a sharp serrated knife, cut bread with a sawing motion into 1-inch-thick diagonal slices. MAKES 6 TO 8 SERVINGS.

Cream Cheese & Chicken Triple Deckers

1 package (3 ounces) cream cheese
2 tablespoons milk
2 tablespoons finely chopped walnuts
Dash of nutmeg
2 cans (5 ounces each) chunk white chicken, cubed
1/3 cup chopped stuffed olives
1/3 cup sour cream
Salt
24 slices Party Pumpernickle Bread
12 slices Party Rye Bread

In a bowl, mash cream cheese and beat in milk, walnuts, and nutmeg. In a second bowl, mix chicken, olives, sour cream, and salt to taste. Spread 12 of the Party Pumpernickle slices with cheese spread; place Party Rye slices on cheese spread. Spread Party Rye slices with chicken spread and top with remaining Party Pumpernickel slices to make triple deckers. Cut sandwiches into halves and spear halves with toothpicks. Wrap and chill until ready to serve.
MAKES 12 SANDWICHES.

French Rolls Mediterranean Style

2 packages (10 ounces each) Brown-and-Serve French
   Rolls
1 can (7 ounces) tuna, drained and flaked
2 tomatoes, chopped
1/2 cup chopped black olives
1 small onion, chopped
1/2 cup minced celery
1 teaspoon salt
1/4 teaspoon pepper
1/2 teaspoon oregano
1/4 cup melted butter or margarine

Split rolls into halves lengthwise. With a sharp knife, scoop out center, leaving shell 1/2-inch thick. Crumble removed roll into bowl. Add remaining ingredients except butter, and mash until well blended. Pile mixture into bottom halves of the rolls. Replace tops and arrange rolls on foil-lined shallow baking pan. Generously brush rolls with butter and bake at 350°F for 30 minutes, or until tops of rolls are brown and crusty. Serve hot, cut into thick slices, or serve whole for a complete meal. These rolls may be stuffed ahead of time and refrigerated. Bake at last minute, after brushing with butter.

MAKES 4 GENEROUS SERVINGS, OR 8 APPETIZER SANDWICH SERVINGS.

Curried Beef Pockets

1 pound ground chuck
1 medium onion, chopped
1 medium apple, peeled, and chopped
1/2 cup raisins
1-1/2 teaspoons salt
1 teaspoon curry powder
1 package (8 ounces) Sandwich Pockets
1 cup (8 ounces) plain yogurt

Cook ground chuck and onion over medium heat until meat is browned and onion is tender. Spoon off excess fat. Add apple, raisins, salt, and curry. Simmer covered for 5 minutes, or until apple is tender. Heat Sandwich Pockets at 400°F for 5 minutes, if desired. Cut a 1/4-inch piece from the top of each Pocket and open. Fill with hot mixture and spoon yogurt over filling. Serve at once.

MAKES 8 SERVINGS.

Greek Meat Pockets

1/4 cup oil
1 onion, finely chopped
1 garlic clove, chopped
1 small eggplant, peeled, and cut into 1-inch cubes
1 large tomato, chopped
1 cup tomato juice
1/4 teaspoon crumbled oregano
Salt and Pepper
3 cups thinly sliced cooked meat (beef, lamb, or pork)
1 package (8 ounces) Sandwich Pockets
1/2 cup finely crumbled feta or farmer cheese

In a skillet, heat oil and sauté onion and garlic for 5 minutes. Add eggplant and tomato and stir over high heat until tomatoes are mushy. Stir in tomato juice and oregano. Add salt and pepper to taste. Cover and simmer for 15 to 20 minutes, or until eggplant is tender and mixture is thick. Add meat and stir over low heat until hot and bubbly. Heat Pockets at 400°F for 5 minutes, if desired. Cut a 1/4-inch piece from the top of each Sandwich Pocket and open. Fill with hot mixture and top with crumbled cheese.

MAKES 8 SERVINGS.

Hot Deviled Ham Croque Monsieur

1 can (4-1/2 ounces) deviled ham
2 tablespoons well-drained pickle relish
1 cup (4 ounces) shredded Swiss cheese
1 teaspoon prepared mustard
8 slices Sandwich White or Toasting White Bread
2 eggs
1 cup milk
1/2 teaspoon salt
1/4 cup butter or margarine

In a bowl, mix ham, relish, cheese, and mustard. Spread mixture on 4 slices of the bread and top with remaining slices of bread. In a shallow dish, beat eggs with milk and salt. Heat butter in a large skillet. Dip sandwiches into egg mixture, coating them on both sides. Place into skillet and fry slowly until richly browned on both sides. Serve hot with cherry tomatoes and green pepper strips.

MAKES 4 SANDWICHES.

Toasted Cheese and Ham Loaf

1 loaf (1 pound) Whole Wheat Bread
16 thin slices boiled ham
1 package (8 ounces) American cheese slices
1/2 cup butter or margarine, melted
1/2 teaspoon garlic powder
2 tablespoons grated Parmesan cheese

Make 8 sandwiches using 2 bread slices, 2 ham slices, and 1 slice of cheese for each sandwich. Spear sandwiches together in the shape of the original loaf using heatproof skewers. Place on a shallow, foil-lined pan. Combine remaining ingredients and spoon over loaf. Open slices to allow butter mixture to run into loaf. Bake at 350°F for 30 to 35 minutes. Pull sandwiches apart and eat hot.
MAKES 8 SERVINGS.

Apple Cheese Logs

1 package (8 ounces) Brown-and- Serve Club Rolls
Butter or margarine
1 can (1 pound, 5 ounces) apple pie filling
1 cup (4 ounces) shredded Cheddar cheese
12 slices partially cooked bacon

Bake Brown-and-Serve Club Rolls according to package directions. Split in half lengthwise and spread with butter. For each serving, cover bottom half with pie filling, then Cheddar cheese, and top with 2 strips of bacon; replace top of roll. Bake at 350°F until cheese melts, filling is heated, and bacon is crisp. Can also be made with peach pie filling.
MAKES 6 SERVINGS.

Deli Delight

1/4 cup mayonnaise
1 teaspoon mustard
1 tablespoon horseradish
8 slices Family Rye Bread
8 slices rare roast beef
1-1/2 cups well-drained prepared coleslaw
8 slices crisp bacon
8 red onion rings

Toasted Cheese and Ham Loaf

In a bowl, mix mayonnaise, mustard, and horseradish. Spread mixture on one side of each slice of bread. Place roast beef slices on 4 of the bread slices. Top with coleslaw, bacon slices, and onion rings. Place remaining slices of bread, mayonnaise side down, on sandwich. Cut sandwiches into halves and serve with celery hearts and radishes.
MAKES 4 SERVINGS.

Tuna Avocado Sandwich

1 ripe avocado, peeled, seeded, and mashed
2 tablespoons minced onion
1 tablespoon lemon juice
1 can (7 ounces) tuna, drained and flaked
1 ripe tomato, cored and chopped
2 tablespoons sunflower seeds
Salt and pepper to taste
8 slices Honey Wheatberry Bread
Leaf lettuce leaves, or shredded Iceberg lettuce

In a bowl, mix avocado, onion, lemon juice, tuna, tomato, and sunflower seeds. Season to taste with salt and pepper. Spread mixture thickly on 4 of the bread slices. Top with lettuce and remaining slices of bread. Serve with mandarin orange sections.
MAKES 4 SANDWICHES.

Zebra Loaf

1/3 cup soft butter or margarine
1 package (1 pound) Mozzarella cheese, shredded
1 package (10 ounces) sharp Cheddar cheese, shredded
1 package (8 ounces) cream cheese
1/2 cup grated Parmesan cheese
8 slices Rye Bread
9 slices Pumpernickel Bread

In a bowl, mix butter and all cheeses. Spread mixture between bread slices alternating rye and pumpernickel slices to make a long striped loaf. Place loaf on a greased piece of foil. Bake at 350°F for 25 to 30 minutes or until cheese is melted and loaf is hot. Cut loaf while hot into diagonal slices so pieces are cut across the striped loaf. Serve hot with pickled cherry peppers, olives, and a tossed green salad.
MAKES 8 TO 10 SERVINGS.

Italian Meat Ball Sandwich

2 loaves (1 pound each) Brown-and-Serve Italian Bread or
    1 package (12 ounces) French Rolls
1/2 pound ground beef
1/2 pound ground pork
1/4 pound ground veal
1 cup soft bread crumbs (from bread centers)
1 egg, well beaten
2 tablespoons water
1 tablespoon grated Parmesan cheese
1 tablespoon minced parsley
1 clove minced garlic
1 teaspoon salt
1/4 teaspoon pepper
2 tablespoons olive oil
1 jar (2 pounds) prepared spaghetti sauce
    with mushrooms
1 tablespoon oregano
2 green peppers, seeded and cut into sixths

Cut each Italian Loaf or French Roll in half horizontally; scoop out bread centers leaving 1/2-inch shells. Place cut side down on cookie sheet and bake according to package directions. Lightly combine meats with next 8 ingredients. Moisten fingers with water and lightly shape mixture into 24 balls. Heat oil in skillet; add meat balls and brown lightly, turning often. Drain off any excess fat. Add sauce and oregano; cover and simmer 30 minutes. Arrange bottom halves of bread or rolls on serving platter. Place meat balls and raw peppers on bread, ladle on sauce and cover with sandwich tops. Serve with antipasto as tasty garnish.
MAKES 6 GENEROUS SERVINGS.

Sausage and Pepper-Filled Deli Rolls

1-1/2 pounds sweet Italian sausage
1 clove garlic, chopped
2 red onions, sliced thinly
2 red peppers, seeded and cut into thin strips
2 green peppers, seeded and cut into thin strips
3 tomatoes, chopped
1 teaspoon oregano
Salt and pepper to taste
1 package (8-1/4 ounces) Sesame Seed Buns

Slice sausages in 1/2-inch-thick crosswise slices. Fry sausage in a skillet until brown and cooked; remove from skillet. Add garlic, onions, and peppers to pan drippings. Sauté for 5 to 6 minutes or until vegetables are tender but still crisp. Add tomatoes and oregano and simmer for 5 to 6 minutes, or until tomatoes are cooked and sauce is thickened. Season to taste with salt and pepper. Split Sesame Seed Buns and fill with sausage filling. Serve at once with plenty of napkins.
MAKES 6 SERVINGS.

Chili Sloppy Joes

1 pound ground beef
1 small onion, chopped
1/3 cup sliced green pepper
1/2 teaspoon chili powder
1/2 teaspoon salt
1/2 teaspoon garlic salt
1 can (16 ounces) tomato sauce
1 can (1 pound, 4 ounces) kidney beans, drained
1 can (8-3/4 ounces) whole kernel corn, drained
1/4 cup sliced green olives
6 English Muffins, split and toasted

Brown beef in large skillet and drain excess fat. Stir in onion and green pepper. Season with chili powder, salt, and garlic salt. Cook several minutes until vegetables are tender. Stir in tomato sauce, kidney beans, corn, and olives. Cook until heated, stirring occasionally. To serve, spoon over toasted English Muffin halves.
MAKES 6 SERVINGS.

Hot Tuna Crunch Muffins

2 cans (7 ounces each) tuna, drained and flaked
1/2 cup finely sliced celery
1/4 cup minced onion
1 tablespoon Worcestershire sauce
1/2 tablespoon pepper
1/2 cup mayonnaise
1/2 cup chopped salted nuts
6 English Muffins
Butter or margarine
12 slices American cheese

Combine tuna, celery, onion, Worcestershire sauce, and pepper. Stir in mayonnaise and nuts. Split English Muffins with a fork. Spread halves with butter and toast under broiler. Spread tuna mixture on muffins; top with slices of cheese; broil until filling is heated through and cheese is melted. Arrange 2 halves on individual plates and serve with a vegetable or fruit salad.

Makes 6 servings.

Hot Ratatouille Roll

2 tablespoons olive oil
1 clove garlic, chopped
1 onion, chopped
1 zucchini, chopped
2 cups diced, peeled eggplant
2 tomatoes, cored and chopped
1/4 teaspoon each basil, oregano, and thyme
Salt and pepper to taste
1-1/2 cups (6 ounces) shredded Mozzarella cheese
1 package (8 ounces) Frankfurter Rolls

In a large skillet, heat oil and sauté garlic and onion for 5 minutes. Stir in zucchini, eggplant, tomatoes, and herbs. Simmer uncovered, stirring occasionally, until mixture is thick, about 15 to 20 minutes. Season to taste with salt and pepper. Shred cheese very coarsely or cut into thin strips. Spoon ratatouille into rolls. Top with Mozzarella cheese. Serve hot with raw mushroom slices.

Makes 6 servings.

Sprouted Wheat Party Loaf

12 slices Sprouted Wheat Bread
1 can (7-3/4 ounces) salmon, drained and flaked
1 hard-cooked egg, finely chopped
1/4 cup mayonnaise
1 tablespoon chopped parsley
1/2 tablespoon minced onion
1-1/4 teaspoons dried dill weed
1 package (8 ounces) cream cheese, softened at
    room temperature
2 to 3 tablespoons milk
Parsley and radish roses for garnish

Remove crusts from bread slices. (If desired, for future use, dry crusts in brown bag; crush for use as bread crumbs.) Set aside. Combine salmon, egg, mayonnaise, parsley, onion, and 1/4 teaspoon dill weed. Mix until smooth. Spread 10 of the bread slices evenly with salmon mixture; keep remaining 2 slices for top. Stack spread slices one on top of the other making 2 stacks, each with 5 slices. Top each stack with plain slices. Press each stack down firmly and wrap with plastic. Refrigerate 30 minutes or longer. Beat cream cheese with milk until smooth and stir in remaining dill. Unwrap chilled stacks and place side-by-side on serving plate. Frost with cream cheese mixture covering entire loaf. Refrigerate 30 minutes. Cut into 8 to 10 servings with sharp knife, keeping loaf intact. Before serving garnish top with bouquet of parsley and radish roses.
MAKES 8 TO 10 SERVINGS.

Wheat Banana Grills

8 slices Whole Wheat Bread
Soft butter or margarine
4 bananas cut into 1/2-inch-thick slices
1/2 cup firmly-packed brown sugar
3 tablespoons soft butter or margarine
3 tablespoons light cream or half-and-half
3 tablespoons smooth peanut butter
1/2 cup chopped peanuts

Spread slices of bread on one side with butter. Place buttered side up on a cookie sheet. Top with banana slices. In a bowl, mix remaining ingredients until well blended. Spread mixture over bananas. Place under broiler until topping is lightly brown and bubbly. Serve warm.
MAKES 8 SERVINGS.

Open Face Pumpernickel Sandwich

8 slices Pumpernickel Bread
Soft butter or margarine
Chopped chives
8 slices boiled or baked ham
2 navel oranges, peeled and sliced
3 carrots, shredded
1/3 cup raisins
Mayonnaise or plain yogurt
4 slices American cheese, each slice cut into 4 strips
    (Swiss, Provolone, or Cheddar may be used)

Toast bread and spread with butter. Sprinkle with chives. Top with ham slices and orange slices. In a bowl, mix carrots, raisins, and enough mayonnaise or yogurt to make a thick mixture. Spoon mixture on orange slices. Top each sandwich with 2 strips of cheese and sprinkle with additional chopped chives. Place under broiler until cheese melts.
MAKES 8 SERVINGS.

Chicken Baskets

6 English Muffins
Melted butter or margarine
1 can (4-3/4 ounces) chicken spread
2 eggs, hard-cooked and chopped
1/2 cup chopped celery
1/2 cup tartar sauce
3 green pepper rings, cut into halves
Radish roses

With a sharp knife, cut out the centers of the muffins, leaving a shell 1/2-inch thick. Crumble removed bread and place into a bowl. Brush shell with melted butter inside and out and place on a cookie sheet. Bake at 400°F for 10 to 15 minutes, or until muffins are lightly browned. Mix crumbled bread with chicken spread, eggs, celery, and tartar sauce. Pile mixture into toasted shells. Press in halved pepper rings to resemble basket handles. Garnish with radish roses. Eat with a knife and fork.
MAKES 6 SERVINGS.

Christmas Sandwich Wreath

DEVILED SPREAD
1 can (4-1/2 ounces) deviled ham
1/4 cup finely chopped celery
1/2 teaspoon Worcestershire sauce
20 slices Party Pumpernickel Bread
Softened butter

CHICKEN APPLE SPREAD
1 can (4-1/2 ounces) chicken spread
1/4 cup chopped, peeled apple
1 tablespoon sour cream
20 slices Party Rye Bread
Softened butter

NIPPY PATE SPREAD
1 can (4-3/4 ounces) liverwurst spread
1/4 cup chopped green pepper
1 tablespoon mayonnaise
20 slices Party Rye Bread
Softened butter

In each recipe combine first 3 ingredients to make 3 separate fillings. Spread 1 side of bread slices with softened butter. Spread half of slices with any of the fillings and close sandwiches with remaining slices. (Each sandwich filling makes 10 sandwiches.) To form wreath, arrange sandwiches, standing on their edges, on the outside edge of a large 12-inch round plate. Decorate wreath with a satin or paper bow.
MAKES 30 SMALL SANDWICHES.

Easy Sandwich Fillings

Cucumber Yogurt: Thin 1 package (3 ounces) cream cheese to spreading consistency with about 1 tablespoon plain yogurt. Season with 1/2 teaspoon minced onion and a dash of salt. Spread on 4 slices buttered Sprouted Wheat Bread. Top with thinly sliced cucumber and 4 more buttered bread slices.
MAKES 4 SANDWICHES.

Grilled Cheese and Pepper: Cover 8 Sprouted Wheat Bread slices with 8 slices Cheddar cheese. Sprinkle with 1 freshly chopped, seeded green pepper. Top with second slice of bread. Toast on both sides on a lightly buttered grill until cheese is melted.
MAKES 8 SANDWICHES.

Chipped Beef and Pineapple: Mince 1 jar (2-1/2 ounces) chipped beef. Combine with 1/4 cup drained crushed pineapple, 1 package (3 ounces) cream cheese and 1 teaspoon horseradish. Make sandwiches using 12 slices Cracked Wheat Bread.
MAKES 6 SANDWICHES.

Farmer Cheese and Pimiento-olive: Combine 1 package (8 ounces) farmer cheese, 2 tablespoons chopped stuffed olives and 1 teaspoon minced onion. Stir in enough sour cream to make a spreadable mixture; add salt to taste. Spread on 4 slices of Pumpernickel Bread. Top with another 4 slices of bread.
MAKES 4 SANDWICHES.

Egg and Green Pepper: Combine 2 chopped hard-cooked eggs, 1 tablespoon chopped green pepper, 1/4 cup sour cream, 1 tablespoon minced scallion, and salt to taste. Spread on 2 slices Cracked Wheat Bread. Top with another 2 slices of bread.
MAKES 2 SANDWICHES.

Party Sandwich Loaf

1 loaf (1 pound) Unsliced White Bread
Soft butter or margarine

HAM FILLING
1 cup minced smoked ham
1/4 cup chopped green pepper
2 tablespoons finely chopped stuffed olives
1/4 cup mayonnaise
2 teaspoons prepared mustard

CHICKEN-EGG SALAD FILLING
1 can (5 ounces) chunk white chicken, cubed
**   or 1 cup cubed cooked chicken**
2 eggs, hard cooked and chopped
1/4 cup finely chopped celery
2 tablespoons minced onion
1/4 teaspoon poultry seasoning
1/4 cup mayonnaise
Salt and pepper to taste

FROSTING
2 packages (8 ounces each) cream cheese, softened at
**   room temperature**
1/4 cup milk
Pimiento strips
Green pepper strips
Green leaves of parsley
Cherry tomatoes

Trim crusts from white bread loaf. Cut loaf into 3 lengthwise slices and butter each slice. In separate bowls, combine and mix ingredients for ham and chicken-egg fillings. Spread first bread slice thickly with chicken mixture; top with second slice, buttered side down. Butter top of slice. Spread thickly with ham mixture; top with third slice, buttered side down. Wrap and chill well. Beat cream cheese and milk until smooth. Frost sides and top of loaf. Garnish with strips of pimiento and green pepper. To serve, place on a platter and decorate with parsley and cherry tomatoes. MAKES IO TO I2 SLICES.

Sandwich Suggestions

CREAM CHEESE SPREAD
1 package (8 ounces) cream cheese, softened
1/3 cup milk

Beat cream cheese until fluffy. Gradually beat in milk to have a smooth spread.

BLUE CHEESE SPREAD
1 cup (1/2 pint) dairy sour cream
1 clove garlic, pressed
1/3 cup finely chopped parsley
1 tablespoon fresh lemon juice
1 tablespoon chopped green onion
1 teaspoon dill weed
1/2 teaspoon salt
1/3 cup crumbled blue cheese

Combine sour cream, garlic, chopped parsley, lemon juice, onion, dill weed, and salt. Blend well. Gently stir in blue cheese. Cover and chill at least 1 hour to allow flavors to blend.

Other Suggestions
Spread slices of White Bread or Very Thin Sliced White or Whole Wheat Bread with either of the above cheese spreads and top with any of the following:

Black olive slices, chopped radishes, shredded carrots, and chopped scallions

Sliced dill pickles topped with chopped scallions

Tomato wedges with shredded lettuce

Pimiento-stuffed green olive slices and celery leaves

Fresh orange slices with halved maraschino cherries

Shredded unpeeled red apple, sliced banana, and halved seedless green grapes

Raw cauliflowerettes, sliced sweet pickles, chopped pimiento, sprinkled with celery salt

Chopped red cabbage, chopped white turnips sprinkled with toasted sesame seeds
Serve sandwiches open face with a knife and fork.
MAKES ENOUGH FOR 8 SANDWICHES.

Desserts

Cherry Jubilee Dessert

1 package (10 ounces) frozen Bake It Fresh Patty Shells
1 can (1 pound) pitted tart red cherries, packed in water
2 tablespoons quick-cooking tapioca
1/2 cup granulated sugar
1/4 teaspoon cinnamon
1/4 teaspoon nutmeg
1/8 teaspoon cloves
1/8 teaspoon salt
1/4 cup water
1 quart rum raisin ice cream

Prepare Patty Shells according to package directions. Drain cherries, reserving liquid. In a saucepan, combine the tapioca, sugar, and spices. Stir in reserved cherry liquid and water; let stand for 5 minutes. Cook, stirring, until mixture just boils. Remove from heat; stir in cherries. Spoon some of this warm sauce into the bottom of baked Patty Shells, add a scoop of ice cream and top with more cherry sauce.
MAKES 6 SERVINGS.

Creamy Pumpkin Bake

1 package (14-1/4 ounces) frozen, Old Fashioned
      Pound Cake
2 eggs, slightly beaten
1-1/2 cups canned pumpkin
3/4 cup firmly packed light brown sugar
1 teaspoon ground cinnamon
1/2 teaspoon ground ginger
1/2 teaspoon ground nutmeg
1/2 teaspoon salt
1/4 teaspoon ground cloves
1 can (13 ounces) evaporated milk

Cut cake into 12 slices. Cut enough slices in half to stand up around the sides of buttered-9 inch square shallow baking dish. Place remaining slices in bottom of baking dish. In a large bowl, combine eggs and pumpkin; add remaining ingredients and blend well. Pour into prepared baking dish. Cover edges of cake crust with foil to prevent excessive browning. Bake at 375° for 50 minutes or until knife inserted in center comes out clean. If desired, garnish with sweetened whipped cream.
Makes 9 servings.

Bordeaux Cheese Torte

1 package (6-3/4 ounces) Bordeaux Cookies
2-1/2 cups unsweetened pineapple juice or orange juice
1/3 cup sugar
2 envelopes unflavored gelatin
1 package (8 ounces) cream cheese
2 cups (1 pint) heavy cream, whipped
1 teaspoon rum flavoring
1 can (1 pound, 4 ounces) pineapple chunks, drained

Use cookies to line the bottom and sides of an ungreased 9-inch spring-form pan. In a saucepan, combine juice, sugar, and gelatin. Stir over low heat until gelatin is dissolved.

In a bowl, beat cream cheese until light and fluffy. Gradually beat in warm gelatin mixture. Chill until mixture mounds when dropped from a spoon. (If mixture accidentally gets too firm, reheat over very low heat to soften.) Fold in whipped cream and rum flavoring.

Carefully pour filling into cookie-lined pan so side cookies remain upright. Chill until firm. Use well-drained pineapple chunks to decorate top of cake. When ready to serve, remove sides of pan and cut into small wedges, between the cookies.

MAKES ONE 8-INCH TORTE.

Pirouettes and Fruits With Champagne

1-1/2 cups sliced fresh peaches
2 tablespoons lemon juice
2 tablespoons water
1 cup fresh pineapple chunks
1 cup halved fresh bing cherries
1 cup seedless green grapes
1 cup strawberries
1/3 cup sugar
Chilled champagne or gingerale
Mint leaves for garnish
1 box (5-1/2) ounces Pirouette Cookies

Peel peaches; slice into lemon juice and water to prevent discoloration. Add remaining fruits and sugar; chill in refrigerator until serving time. Arrange fruits in long-stemmed sherbet glasses. Fill glasses with champagne or ginger ale. Garnish with mint leaves. Serve with cookies.

MAKES 6 SERVINGS.

Mincemeat Cookie Dessert

6 tablespoons cornstarch
1/2 cup sugar
3 cups milk
1 tablespoon vanilla
1/2 cup chopped walnuts
2 packages (7-1/4 ounces each) Chessmen Cookies
1 jar (1 pound, 4-1/2 ounces) prepared mincemeat

In a saucepan, mix cornstarch and sugar. Stir in milk. Cook over medium heat, stirring constantly, until pudding thickens and bubbles. Cool covered. Fold in vanilla and walnuts. Cover and chill.

Place 1/3 of the cookies in the bottom of an 8-inch square pan. Spread with half of the mincemeat and then with half of the pudding. Repeat layering, ending with cookies. Chill several hours. Serve topped with whipped cream or vanilla ice cream. Spoon into dishes to serve.
MAKES 6 TO 8 SERVINGS.

Yogurt-Peach Chocolate Delight

4 squares semi-sweet chocolate
3 tablespoons water
2 egg yolks
2 tablespoons sugar
1 package (12-3/4 ounces) frozen Old Fashioned
    Apple-Walnut Cake
1 can (29 ounces) cling peach halves
1 cup (1/2 pint) Plain Yogurt

In top of double boiler, over simmering water, melt chocolate and water. Stir in egg yolks and stir briskly until mixture thickens; stir in sugar. Cut cake into 6 thick slices. Top each with a peach half, several spoonfuls of chocolate sauce and a dollop of yogurt.
MAKES 6 SERVINGS.

Mincemeat Cookie
Dessert

Cinnamon Raisin Crunch

3 large cooking apples, cored and sliced
1/2 small lemon, thinly sliced and seeded
1/2 cup sugar
1/3 cup chopped pecans
2 tablespoons wheat germ
6 slices Raisin with Cinnamon Bread
1/4 cup butter or margarine
1/3 cup sugar
1/2 teaspoon nutmeg

In a saucepan, combine apples, lemon, and sugar. Simmer covered until apples are tender, about 15 to 20 minutes. Pour into a serving dish and top with pecans and wheat germ. Toast bread on one side under broiler. In a bowl, mix butter, sugar, and nutmeg. Spread mixture on untoasted side of bread. Broil until sugar mixture bubbles and is lightly browned. Place bread sugar-side up on serving plates. Top with some of the warm apples. MAKES 6 SERVINGS.

Candied Fruit Trifle

1/3 cup cornstarch
1/2 cup sugar
3 cups half-and-half
1 tablespoon vanilla
Dash of nutmeg
1 package (10-3/4 ounces) frozen Old Fashioned Pound
     Cake
1/2 cup Cream Sherry
1/2 cup minced candied fruit
Sweetened whipped cream for garnish
Candied cherries for garnish

In a saucepan, combine cornstarch, sugar, and half-and-half. Stir over low heat until thickened and bubbly. Stir in vanilla and nutmeg. Cover and chill.

Cut cake into 10 slices; cut each slice into thirds. Arrange 8 to 10 pieces around edge of 1-1/2-quart dessert dish. Cut remaining slices into cubes. Drizzle cake with Sherry. Fold cake cubes and candied fruit into pudding. Spoon into prepared dessert dish. Chill until ready to serve. Garnish with whipped cream and cherries.
MAKES 6 TO 8 SERVINGS.

Pineapple Fluff Pie

1 Deep Dish, Frozen, Pie Shell
2 envelopes unflavored gelatin
1 can (1 pound, 4 ounces) crushed pineapple,
    undrained
1 cup (1/2 pint) plain yogurt
1 cup (1/2 pint) heavy cream, whipped
1 can (8-1/4 ounces) pineapple slices, drained and
    cut into halves

Bake pie shell as directed on a package for a single crust pie. Cool. Stir gelatin into pineapple and stir over low heat until gelatin is dissolved. Chill until slightly thickened. Fold in yogurt and whipped cream. Pour mixture into baked pie shell. Garnish edge of pie with halved pineapple slices. Chill until firm.
MAKES 1 — 9-INCH PIE.

Walnut Chiffon Pie

1 Deep Dish, Frozen, Pie Shell
2/3 cup firmly packed brown sugar
1 envelope unflavored gelatin
1/2 teaspoon salt
4 egg yolks, beaten
1 cup milk
1 teaspoon vanilla
4 egg whites
Butter-Browned Walnuts*

Bake pie shell according to package directions for a single crust pie. In top of double boiler, combine 1/3 cup of brown sugar gelatin and salt. Add egg yolks and milk. Cook and stir over hot, not boiling water, until mixture is slightly thick. Remove from heat; add vanilla. Chill, stirring occasionally, until mixture mounds when spooned.

Beat egg whites until soft peaks form. Gradually beat in remaining brown sugar, beating to form stiff peaks. Fold in gelatin mixture, then 1/2 cup of the Butter-Browned Walnuts. Pour into baked pie shell. Chill. At serving time, top with remaining walnuts.
MAKES 8 SERVINGS.

*Butter-Browned Walnuts: Toast 1 cup chopped walnuts in 2 tablespoons butter in skillet, stirring frequently. Drain; cool.

Frozen Peach Melba Pirouette Cake

1 package (5-1/2 ounces) Chocolate-Laced Pirouette
    Cookies
1 quart vanilla ice cream
1 can (17 ounces) cling peach slices, drained
3/4 cup raspberry preserves
1/4 cup brandy
1/4 cup slivered toasted almonds

With a sharp knife, using a sawing motion, cut cookies into halves, crosswise. Line the bottom and sides of a 9-inch layer cake pan with foil. Spread ice cream, with a spatula, in an even layer on bottom of pan. Press cookies, cut-side down, around outer edge of pan into ice cream. Press remaining cookies into top of ice cream. Top with peaches. Combine remaining ingredients, mix well, and spoon evenly over peaches. Freeze covered. To serve, use foil to pull cake out of pan. Strip away foil and place on serving platter. Cut into wedges while frozen, and let thaw 10 to 15 minutes.
MAKES 6 TO 8 SERVINGS.

Frozen Orange Cake

2 bags (5 ounces each) Gingerman Cookies
1 envelope unflavored gelatin
1 can (6 ounces) frozen concentrated orange juice,
    thawed and undiluted
2 cups (1 pint) heavy cream, whipped
1/2 cup finely chopped pecans
1/2 cup finely chopped maraschino cherries
Whipped cream and cherries for garnish

Line a 9-inch square pan (2 inches deep) with foil, allowing excess to hang over sides. Use enough of the cookies to line sides and bottom of pan. In a saucepan, mix gelatin and orange juice. Stir over low heat until gelatin is dissolved. Chill until mixture is cold but not thickened. Fold in cream, pecans, and cherries. Spoon half of the cream mixture into pan. Top with remaining cookies and remaining cream mixture.

Freeze until hard. Remove from pan using excess foil to pull out cake. Cut into serving-size pieces while still frozen. Let stand 20 minutes before serving. Garnish with whipped cream and cherries.
MAKES ONE 9-INCH SQUARE CAKE.

Pineapple-Honey Wheatberry Bread Pudding

3 tablespoons melted butter or margarine
8 slices Honey Wheatberry Bread, cut into 1/2-inch
     cubes
2 tablespoons sugar
1 teaspoon ground cinnamon
4 eggs, separated
2 cups milk
1/2 cup shredded coconut
1 cup sugar
1 teaspoon vanilla extract
1 can (1 pound, 4 ounces) pineapple slices, drained

Mix butter, bread cubes, sugar, and cinnamon. Place in bottom of well-greased 1-1/2-quart baking dish. Beat egg yolks with milk. Stir in coconut, 1/2 cup of the sugar, and vanilla. Pour milk mixture over bread cubes. Bake in pan containing 1 inch of hot water at 350°F for 40 minutes.

Remove from oven and arrange pineapple slices on custard. Beat egg whites until stiff. Gradually beat in remaining 1/2 cup sugar, 1 tablespoon at a time. Continue beating until mixture holds stiff peaks. Spread over top of pineapple slices. Return to oven and bake for 15 minutes longer, or until meringue is golden brown. Serve warm, or at room temperature. Can also be made with Honey Bran Bread and 3 cups sliced fresh or frozen peaches.
MAKES 6 TO 8 SERVINGS.

Banana Coconut Bake

1 package (12-3/4 ounces) frozen Old Fashioned,
     Pound Cake, cubed
2 large ripe bananas, sliced
1 cup (3-1/2 ounce can) flaked coconut
4 eggs, slightly beaten
4 cups milk
1-1/2 teaspoons vanilla extract
1/8 teaspoon salt

In a 1-1/2 quart buttered baking dish, alternate layers of cake cubes, bananas and coconut, ending with coconut. Beat remaining ingredients. Pour mixture into baking dish. Bake at 350° for 50 minutes or until golden and set. Remove from oven and cool on wire rack.
MAKES 6 TO 8 SERVINGS.

Apricot Swoons

1 package (17-1/4 ounces) frozen Bake It Fresh Puff
  Pastry
1/2 cup thick apricot preserves
1 cup ground almonds (grind in blender or food
  processor)
1 teaspoon almond extract
1/4 cup grated semi-sweet chocolate
Dash salt
1 egg, beaten slightly
Sliced almonds

Thaw puff pastry 20 minutes, then unfold. On a lightly floured board, roll each sheet to a 12 inch square, then cut each sheet into 16 — 3 inch squares; brush with beaten egg.

Combine next five ingredients. Place about a teaspoonful of apricot mixture on each square and fold over into triangles. Seal by pressing edges together with flour-dipped fork tines. Place approximately 1 inch apart on ungreased baking sheet, prick with fork tines, brush with egg and if desired, top with almonds. Bake in preheated hot oven (400°) until puffed and golden, approximately 8 minutes.
MAKES 32 TRIANGLES.

Apricot-Banana Refrigerator Cake

1 package (14-1/4 ounces) frozen Old Fashioned
  Pound cake
2 packages (3 ounces each) orange gelatin
2 cups boiling orange juice
2 cups (1 pint) sour cream
1 can (17 ounces) apricot halves, drained and diced
2 ripe bananas, sliced

Cut thawed cake into 14 thin slices and use slices to line the bottom and sides of an ungreased 9 x 5 x 3 inch loaf pan. Stand slices on side to line pan. Dissolve gelatin in boiling orange juice. Beat in sour cream. Chill until mixture thickens slightly. Fold in apricots and bananas. Pour mixture into lined pan. Trim cake slices even with pan. Place trimmed pieces into gelatin mixture. Chill until firm. Unmold cake onto a serving platter. Cut into slices to serve.
MAKES 1 — 9 INCH LOAF CAKE.

Chocolate Banana Tarts

3/4 cup milk
1 tablespoon cornstarch
1 package (6 ounces) semi-sweet chocolate pieces
2 eggs
3 tablespoons strong coffee*
2 tablespoons rum
**2 packages (10 ounces each) frozen Bake It Fresh Patty
    Shells**
2 cups (about 3 medium) sliced bananas

In a small saucepan, mix milk and cornstarch. Cook, stirring, until thickened. Pour into blender container. Add chocolate pieces, eggs, coffee, and rum. Cover and process at high speed for 3 minutes. Mixture will be thin. Pour into bowl and chill for 4 hours. Bake Patty Shells according to package directions; cool. When ready to serve, peel and slice bananas. Fold into the chocolate mixture and spoon into Patty Shells.
MAKES 12 TARTS.

*Or 3 tablespoons water and 1/2 teaspoon instant coffee powder.

Baklava

**2 packages (10 ounces each) frozen Bake It Fresh Patty
    Shells, thawed in wrappings overnight**
3 cups finely chopped walnuts or pecans
Grated rind of one lemon
1 cup honey, warmed
Whipped cream (optional)

Line a 9 x 9 x 2-inch baking pan with foil. Place 3 Patty Shells one on top of the other and roll out to a 9-inch square. Repeat with remaining Patty Shells. You will have 4 (9-inch) squares. Place 1 sheet in bottom of baking pan. Mix walnuts and lemon rind. Sprinkle pastry with 1/3 of the walnut mixture, and drizzle with 1/4 of the honey. Repeat process 3 times, making the top layer plain pastry and reserving 1/4 cup of the honey. With the tip of a sharp knife, cut diagonal lines 1/8-inch deep in top of pastry. Bake in a preheated hot oven (400°F) for 30 to 35 minutes. Let cool slightly in pan. Drizzle surface with last of the honey. Remove from pan and peel away foil. Cut into diamonds or tiny 1-1/2-inch squares. Serve with more honey, or whipped cream if desired.
MAKES 12 SERVINGS.

Individual Napoleons

1 package (17-1/4 ounces) frozen Bake It Fresh Puff
    Pastry
4 squares (4 ounces) semi-sweet chocolate
1 cup (1/2 pint) sour cream
1/2 cup sweet butter
1 cup confectioners' sugar
1 tablespoon brandy
Chocolate curls

Thaw puff pastry 20 minutes, then unfold. Cut each square into halves, then cut each half crosswise into 5 two-inch wide strips. You will have 20 strips. Bake strips on an ungreased baking sheet in a preheated moderate oven (350°) for 18 to 20 minutes.

    Melt chocolate over very low heat. Stir in sour cream and butter. Cool until thickened. Generously spoon pudding on half of the pastry pieces and top with the other half. Blend sugar and brandy. Drizzle over top of Napoleons and top with chocolate curls. To prepare chocolate curls, shave chocolate, warmed to room temperature, with a vegetable peeler.

MAKES 10 NAPOLEONS.

Quick Dobos Torte

1 package (10-3/4 ounces) frozen Old Fashioned Pound
    Cake
1/2 cup butter or margarine, softened
6 squares (6 ounces) semi-sweet chocolate, melted and
    cooled
1 egg yolk
2 teaspoons brandy
Sliced almonds for garnish

With a sharp knife, cut cake into 7 thin, lengthwise layers. Combine remaining ingredients except sliced almonds and beat until thick and spreadable. It may be necessary to chill slightly. Place 1 layer on a serving platter; spread very thinly with frosting. Repeat until all layers are stacked. Frost top and sides of cake. Sprinkle top with sliced almonds. Refrigerate until ready to serve. Cut cake into thin slices while chilled. If frosting thickens, place over low heat and stir until spreadable again.

MAKES 8 SERVINGS.

Berry Crème Glacé in Patty Shells

1 package (10 ounces) frozen Bake It Fresh Patty Shells
1 package (3-1/4 ounces) vanilla pudding
1-1/2 cups light cream
2 tablespoons butter
1 teaspoon vanilla
18 whole strawberries, washed and hulled
1/3 cup melted currant jelly

Prepare Patty Shells according to package directions. Meanwhile, cook pudding according to package directions using only 1-1/2 cups of light cream, 2 tablespoons butter, and 1 teaspoon vanilla for extra creamy richness. Place sheet of plastic wrap directly on pudding surface to prevent formation of hard crust. Cool. When ready to serve, heap Patty Shells with pudding. Top each Shell with 3 strawberries and glaze by drizzling melted and slightly cooled currant jelly over berries. Raspberries or blueberries can be used instead of strawberries.
MAKES 6 SERVINGS.

Buttermilk Berry Pie

1-1/2 cups Sprouted Wheat Bread crumbs
1/4 cup melted butter or margarine
1 tablespoon sugar
1/2 cup sugar
1/3 cup cornstarch
2 cups buttermilk
1 teaspoon vanilla
1/2 teaspoon nutmeg
2 cups fresh berries or drained apricot halves
1/2 cup apricot preserves, heated

Dry 6 slices (or enough to make 1-1/2 cups crumbs) of bread in a 350°F oven for 15 to 20 minutes, and crumble in a blender, or with a rolling pin. Add butter or margarine and 1 tablespoon sugar; mix well. Pat this mixture into bottom and sides of a 9-inch pie pan. In a saucepan, mix sugar and cornstarch. Stir in buttermilk. Cook, stirring, over medium heat until pudding bubbles and thickens. Cool. Fold in vanilla and nutmeg. Pour into pie crust. Chill. When ready to serve, top with berries. Heat preserves and spoon over berries. Serve at once. This pie shell is good for any favorite filling, cream or chiffon.
MAKES 6 TO 8 SERVINGS.

Cooking without recipes

The bakers at Pepperidge Farm have done all the hard work for you. Now for all the home-makers who clip recipes but never use them, here are plenty of quick ideas that can be used without recipes for breakfast, lunch, or for a quick snack. Enjoy our tour through the edible world of Pepperidge Farm.

BREADS

Toast *Corn & Molasses* bread slices. Top with a thin slice of cheese and creamy scrambled eggs sprinkled with chopped tomatoes for a quick breakfast or lunch.

Trim crusts from slices of *Honey Bran Bread*. Spread with liverwurst spread, add a small strip of cheese or pickle, and roll up. Wrap in wax paper and chill.

Trim crusts from *Oatmeal Bread* and cut into small triangles. Dip into melted butter and then into grated Parmesan cheese. Bake at 350°F for 10 to 15 minutes, or until golden. Mix with salted nuts as a snack, or add to cream soups or onion soup.

Party Slices of *Rye* or *Pumpernickel* are great for weight watchers. Eating 2 or 3 slices seems naughty but has less calories than regular loafs. Instead of breakable potato chips, toast party slices and use them as dippers.

Make your next bread pudding or turkey stuffing using *Raisin with Cinnamon Bread*. Add crumbled Raisin Bread to your favorite meatloaf mixture instead of the usual bread. If you are tired of the usual breakfast cereals, toast cubes of Raisin Bread, pop them into a cereal bowl, and top with milk.

Make school sandwiches of *Family Rye* for a whole week using freezable fillings such as chicken or egg salad, cheese, meat, or peanut butter. Wrap and freeze. Sandwiches thaw in lunch box and remain cold and fresh for a long time.

Spread slices of *Pumpernickel* thinly with chive cream cheese. Stack 3 slices and top with a plain slice. Wrap tightly and chill. Cut into 1/2-inch-wide strips and then cut strips into bite-size pieces to make a fast tea sandwich or cocktail snack.

Dry any leftover *Seedless Rye* slices and crush into crumbs with a rolling pin, blender, or food processor. Use as breading for chicken, fish, veal, etc., for a subtle rye-flavor crust.

Toast slices of *Jewish Rye*. Spread lightly with mustard mixed with horseradish. Top with thin slices of beef, chicken, lamb, or pork. Heat canned beef or chicken gravy with a little red or white wine. Add some instant minced onion, some sliced olives, and chopped pickles, and pour over meat. Serve with a knife and fork.

For that boring diet, add the flavor of *Very Thin Rye* spread thinly with low-fat cottage cheese mixed with a little prepared mustard and chopped celery served with clear broth for a welcome snack.

Trim crusts from *Unsliced White*. Cut block of bread remaining crosswise and lengthwise into 8 square pieces, cutting not quite all the way through. Brush heavily with melted butter mixed with garlic powder and chives. Sprinkle with grated Parmesan cheese and bake at 400°F for 15 to 20 minutes, or until brown. Break apart to serve.

Very Thin Sliced is another low calorie bread for weight watchers. Toast to make your own Melba toast.

Dry out any leftover *White With Cracked Wheat* slices and crumble finely. Add crumbs to thicken soups, sauces, or stews instead of flour. Sprinkle in crumbs a little at a time until the desired thickness is reached. Adds flavor and texture.

Slice *Sourdough Round Loaf* horizontally into 3 or 4 slices. Spread with your favorite filling. Restack slices in original loaf and cut into wedges to serve.

Toast and cut any of the *Wheat Bread*s into cubes and use to top fish fillets, casseroles, pot pies, or any creamy food that is baked. Adds more flavor and whole grain nutrients.

Very Thin Whole Wheat is another calorie-counter bonanza. Top slices with thin tomato slices sprinkled with dill. Add a low-fat cheese slice and grill for a quick, low-calorie, nourishing lunch.

French Bread can be cut into 1-inch thick slices, cutting not quite all the way through. Sauté 1 chopped onion in butter until golden. Spread mixture in cuts. Brush loaf with butter and sprinkle with grated Cheddar cheese. Bake at 350°F for 15 to 20 minutes, or until toasted. Pull apart to serve.

SWEET

Spread slices of *Cracked Wheat* with butter on both sides. Place half the slices on a cookie sheet and top with spoonfuls of any fruit pie filling. Top with second slice and bake at 350°F for 20 to 30 minutes, or until crisp. Serve with vanilla ice cream.

Honey Wheatberry slices could be cut into 1/2-inch cubes. Brown cubes in butter until golden. Sprinkle with cinnamon sugar and sprinkle on top of a bowl of applesauce or warm pudding.

Toast slices of *Wheat Germ* bread and spread with a thin layer of mincemeat or your favorite preserves. Sprinkle with chopped nuts. Prepare butterscotch pudding as directed on package and spoon while warm over mincemeat.

Toasting White slices can be cut into 3 pieces to shape fingers. Dip each finger into sweetened condensed milk and then roll in coconut. Bake on a greased cookie sheet at 350°F for 7 to 10 minutes. Serve warm.

Spread slices of toasted *Sprouted Wheat* bread with butter and sprinkle with brown sugar and a dusting of nutmeg and grated orange rind.

ROLLS

Hollow out the 2-inch long *French Rolls* and fill with your favorite chicken or tuna salad. Brush rolls with melted butter and bake at 350°F for 15 to 20 minutes. Serve hot, sprinkled with crumbled crisp bacon.

Fill *Hamburger Buns* with hot, cooked, frozen breaded fish fillets or fish sticks; top with American cheese slices and tartar sauce. Or top with sizzling hot Canadian bacon, hard-cooked egg, and cheese slices.

Open *Parker House Rolls* and pop in a grilled cocktail frank. Add mustard and a few slivers of scallion.

Brush *Sesame Seed Buns* with melted butter and dust with onion, garlic, or celery salt. Warm at 300°F for a few minutes.

Split *Soft Family Rolls* and fill with thinly-sliced smoked ham and mustard and sweet pickle relish.

Split *Golden Twist Rolls* and spread with softened cream cheese. Top with sweetened sliced strawberries. Replace top and brown as directed. Can be served warm topped with whipped cream.

For that elegant dinner, split *Butter Crescent Rolls* and spread with liver pâté, chopped chives, and a few canned mushroom slices. Close and warm at 300°F for 5 to 6 minutes. Serve warm as an appetizer with a clear consommé.

Fill *Frankfurter Rolls* with a slice of ham topped with scrambled eggs for an easy-eating breakfast for the kids.

SWEET

For a snack, spread a *Frankfurter Roll* with peanut butter and top with a few spoons of vanilla ice cream.

Pour any flavor canned fruit pie filling into a casserole. Top with *Old-Fashioned Rolls*. Splash with melted butter, sugar, and cinnamon or nutmeg. Bake at 350°F for 20 to 25 minutes, or until bubbly.

For a quick Danish pastry, split *Dinner Rolls* and spread with apricot preserves mixed with slivered toasted almonds. Close roll and drizzle top with confectioners sugar, mixed with orange juice to a thick, creamy consistency.

BROWN-AND-SERVE BREADS AND ROLLS

Spread *Brown-and-Serve Italian Bread* with soft butter mixed with a little fines herbes and instant minced onion. Bake as usual.

Bake *Brown-and-Serve Italian Bread* as usual. When brown, slice lengthwise, top one half with thin slices of prosciutto and thin slices of Mozzarella cheese. Top with other half. Bake until cheese melts. Cut into thin crosswise slices to serve.

Brown-and-Serve Club Rolls can be brushed with beaten egg and sprinkled with coarse salt, or sesame, poppy, caraway, or dill seeds. Bake as directed.

Brown-and-Serve Hearth Rolls can be brushed with beaten egg and sprinkled with dehydrated onions and poppy seeds. Bake as directed.

Split *Brown-and-Serve Sesame French Style Rolls with Seeds* and fill with slices of Swiss cheese and strips of crisp bacon. Bake as directed.

Cut *Brown-and-Serve French Style Sour Dough Rolls* into 4 crosswise slices but do not cut all the way through. Fill cuts with shrimp or crabmeat salad. Bake as directed.

SANDWICH POCKET SNACK IDEAS

Split *Sandwich Pockets* into 2 thin rounds. Place rough-side up on a cookie sheet. Spoon on a layer of pizza or tomato sauce. Sprinkle with oregano and shredded Mozzarella and Parmesan cheese. Broil until cheese melts for a quick pizza.

Cut *Sandwich Pockets* in half crosswise and open. Fill with desired filling:

Nonsweet Fillings
Slices of cheese, cold cuts with coleslaw, or sliced tomatoes.
Salmon, egg, or chicken salad, with lettuce leaves and shredded carrots.
Ham slices, orange or pineapple slices, and blue cheese with butter spread inside bread.
Slices of cheese with chopped green or red pepper, or sweet chilies, and heated in oven until cheese melts.
Leftover turkey slices with leftover stuffing and vegetables, toasted and then served with leftover gravy spooned over sandwich. For knife and fork.

Sweet Fillings
Frozen yogurt topped with fresh fruits or berries.
A quick banana split—banana halves topped with whipped cream, fudge sauce, and nuts.

Sour cream mixed with brown sugar and topped with fruit or dried fruits.

Fresh strawberries, raspberries, blueberries, or peaches and whipped cream.

For a quick cinnamon toast, breads may also be brushed with melted butter or margarine and sprinkled with sugar mixed with cinnamon and heated.

MUFFINS

Split *Sourdough English Muffins* and make sandwiches with a thick layer of grated Cheddar cheese, some chopped pecans, and a splash of red wine. Bake sandwiches at 350°F for 10 to 15 minutes, or until cheese melts. Cut each sandwich into quarters and serve with your favorite soup or salad.

Split *White English Muffins* into halves and dip into French toast batter of milk and eggs. Brown in butter as usual and serve hot with orange marmalade or maple syrup.

Toast split *Cinnamon-Raisin English Muffins* and top with heated canned apple pie filling. Add vanilla ice cream or whipped cream.

Scoop out *Cinnamon-Apple English Muffins* leaving a shell 1/2-inch thick. Crumble removed muffin and fry in butter until crisp. Fill muffins with chocolate pudding. Sprinkle with crisp muffin crumbs.

CROUTONS

Cheddar & Romano Croutons can be mixed into your favorite dumpling dough. Prepare as usual.

Cheese & Garlic Croutons are delicious sprinkled over a fresh orange and red onion salad.

Top grilled tomato halves with *Onion & Garlic Croutons* before baking.

Seasoned Croutons can be folded into seasoned mashed potatoes for added flavor and crunch. Great also for baked potatoes.

Sour Cream & Chive Croutons can be sprinkled over vegetable casseroles, or any cooked vegetables, such as cauliflower, carrots, cabbage, or broccoli.

WHAT TO DO WITH LEFTOVER COOKED STUFFING

Spoon stuffing into large stemmed mushroom caps. Bake at 350°F for about 10 minutes.

Mix with ground beef and use to stuff peppers or large onions, or make meatloaf or Salisbury steaks.

Use stuffing to line a casserole. Fill with creamed chicken, turkey, or ham and bake as usual.

Shape leftover stuffing into patties and brown on both sides in butter. Serve instead of potatoes or noodles.

Fold leftover cooked vegetables into *Pan Style Stuffing* or add drained canned mushrooms, or chopped fresh tomato for added interest and flavor. Chopped nuts, or the cooked giblets from poultry, or chopped apple or orange can all be added to *Pan Style Stuffing*.

WHAT TO DO WITH LEFTOVER DRY STUFFING MIX

Herb Seasoned Noodles: Mix cooked noodles with *Herb Seasoned Stuffing* sautéed in butter. Allow 1 tablespoon stuffing crumbs sautéed in 1 tablespoon butter for each cup of noodles.

Scrambled Eggs: Sauté *Herb Seasoned Stuffing* in butter before adding egg mixture. Plan on 1 tablespoon of crumbs for each egg.

Casserole Topping: Stuffing crumbs mixed with melted butter couldn't be easier or more tasty.

Salad Croutons: Sauté 1 cup *Herb Seasoned Cube Stuffing* in 2 tablespoons butter. Remove from pan and sprinkle with Parmesan cheese before adding to tossed green salad.

BISCUITS

Chocolate-Laced Pirouettes can be filled, using a pastry bag, with whipped cream or pudding or jelly. Ends can also be dipped into frosting and then into chopped nuts, coconut, or colored or chocolate sprinkles.

Plain Pirouettes can be drizzled with confectioners sugar mixed with milk and sprinkled with chopped nuts or coconut. They can also be frosted with melted chocolate and rolled in nuts, crushed peppermint candy, or coconut.

All the *Cookie Assortment*s are so good and so varied that serving them beautifully arranged on a platter is enough. But if you want to gild the lily, try a European-style coup — plenty of good ice cream in a lovely glass dish, topped with crushed sweetened fruit, with 1 or 2 cookies stuck into the top of the ice cream.

Spread *Bordeaux* cookies with melted chocolate and sandwich 2 together, pressing to make chocolate ooze out of sandwich. Press edge into finely chopped nuts. This can also be done with thick preserves, whipped cream, cheese, or frosting.

Prepare your favorite brownie recipe or mix and spread in pan. Top with *Chessmen* and bake as usual.

Hide a *Capri* cookie in warm Vanilla pudding, spooned into individual serving dishes. Chill until ready to serve.

Add *Cinnamon Sugar* cookies to your next batch of fresh, hot applesauce, or crumble and use to fill baked apples.

Use *Fudge Chip* cookies to make mini-ice cream sandwiches to keep in the freezer for the children.

Decorate *Gingerman* cookies with faces using purchased tubes of frosting. Add aprons, pants, hair, and ruffles with frosting. Sprinkle with colored sugar.

Crumble *Irish Oatmeal* cookies into a bowl. Add raisins and top with stewed fruit such as apples, peaches, apricots, berries, pears, etc.

Line a pie plate with *Lemon Nut Crunch* cookies and fill with packaged lemon pie filling, prepared as directed. Chill and top with meringue as directed on package. Bake as directed on package.

Crumble *Molasses Crisps* coarsely and dip your ice cream cones into crumbs. Or scoop ice cream and roll balls in crumbs and freeze until needed. Serve balls topped with fudge or butterscotch sauce.

Place a *Lido Cookie* on a cling peach half on a cookie sheet. Top with meringue, covering cookie completely. Bake at 350°F for 10 to 12 minutes, or until golden brown.

Place a *Milano Cookie* on a slice of vanilla or peach ice cream. When ready to serve, top with hot chocolate pudding.

Top a serving of orange sherbet with a *Nassau Cookie*. Drizzle with orange marmalade mixed with rum flavoring.

Top drained canned pear halves with a little Cointreau or Amaretto and *Orleans*

Cookies, chocolate side up. Place under broiler until chocolate melts. Serve with whipped cream.

Serve *Tahiti Cookies* around a tropical ambrosia made of fresh orange slices, diced fresh pineapple, banana slices, and toasted coconut.

Kitchen Hearth Cookies can be sandwiched with chocolate or vanilla frosting. Or they can be frosted on top and sprinkled with nuts, coconut, or grated rinds.

Old-Fashioned Cinnamon Sugar Cookies can be crumbled and sprinkled over your next apple pie before baking instead of another crust.

Brownie Chocolate Nut Cookies can be sandwiched with peanut butter, peach preserves, or mint jelly.

Drizzle *Chocolate Chip Cookies* with coffee frosting and sprinkle very lightly with crushed instant coffee.

Use *Peanut Cookies* polka-dot style over your next frosted layer cake or sheet cake.

Cut *Oatmeal Raisin Cookies* into halves. Press halves, rounded sides together to resemble a butterfly, into tops of frosted cupcakes.

Make your next trifle using layers of *Shortbread Cookies* instead of cake.

Crumble *Sugar Cookies* finely. Brush chunks of banana with honey and roll in crumbs. Pile in serving dishes and drizzle with marshmallow or fudge sauce for an instant banana split. Add ice cream, if you wish.

Goldfish crackers are delicious served over salads, soups, sauces, or any mushy food that needs flavor and crunch. Can also be crumbled for a casserole topping or breading for fish, poultry, etc.

Goldfish Thins can be served as scoopers and dippers. Can also be made into sandwiches using deviled ham, tuna, creamy cheeses, or liver pâté. Can serve as sandwiches, open face and prettily garnished. Fill thins just before serving to prevent sogginess.

Wrap *Snack Sticks* in ham or Swiss cheese for a quick pick-up snack or lunch.

Mixed Suits are all great for those munching combinations for TV viewing. Mix with nuts, dried fruits, seeds.

FROZEN DESSERTS

Splash frozen *Apple Dumplings* with a little Sherry, then bake as directed.

Bake *Patty Shells* and store in an air-tight container in a cool, dry place until needed.

For the more ambitious cook, thaw *Patty Shells* in package in refrigerator overnight. Stack 2 of the shells and roll out to an 8-inch round. Repeat with remaining shells. Bake in preheated hot oven (400°F) for 20 to 25 minutes, or until puffed and brown. Spread thick vanilla pudding on 2 of the sheets. Stack sheets and top with plain sheet. Mix confectioners sugar with enough Amaretto to make a thick mixture. Spread over top of torte. Sprinkle with sliced almonds. An easy, glamorous torte for your next party.

Regular *Pie Shells* can be thawed and used to cover deep dish fruit pies or casseroles.

For a tea-time sweet pastry, flatten *Pie Shells* after thawing and spread with soft butter. Sprinkle with sugar and cinnamon and roll up like a jelly roll. Cut into 1/2-inch thick slices and place outside-up on a greased cookie sheet. Bake in preheated moderate oven (375°F) for 10 to 15 minutes, or until brown and crisp. Remove at once and cool on racks.

For this one exception — a recipe for the construction of the cake is needed:

Wedding Cake

6 frozen Vanilla Layer Cakes
1 can (16-1/2 ounces) vanilla frosting
1 teaspoon rum flavoring
Wedding ornament (your own or ready made)
Artificial or fresh flowers

Place 4 of the cakes while frozen in a square on a 16-inch square serving platter or other flat surface. Place remaining 2 cakes, one on top of the other, in the center of the cake square. Allow frosting to thaw slightly. With a wet knife or spatula, smooth all seams of cake to conceal joinings. In a bowl, mix frosting and rum. Place mixture in a pastry bag fitted with a star tip. Press rosettes of frosting to form a continuous row on edge of both cake layers. Chill until ready to serve.

Press wedding ornament on top of cake and, if desired, press rosettes or artificial flowers around bottom of ornament. Decorate cake layers and base with artificial or fresh washed and dried flowers.

To cut cake, start cutting at the top tier. Cut into small squares for each serving. When top tier is cut, then cut bottom tier into small squares. MAKES 60 SERVINGS.

COOKING WITHOUT RECIPES WITH FROZEN LAYER CAKES

Decorate-a-Cake Birthday Party
Come to my party next Friday at eight
The fun will start early so don't dare to be late.
Although it's my birthday the surprise is for you
To learn what I've planned come see what we do.

Karen's birthday invitation *was* a bit unusual, but then, so was her party idea. She wanted to do something different for her eleven-year-old friends who had been to dozens of parties and were on the verge of outgrowing the usual birthday games. A trip to the hamburger stand or the bowling alley crossed her mind, but that really wasn't it — there had to be something new; something no one else had done before. She'd have the *first* Decorate-a-Cake Birthday Party! All the girls had seen and eaten decorated birthday cakes, but how many had decorated cakes of their own?

She made a list of everything she'd need: A cake for each girl (store-bought Pepperidge Farm frozen layer cakes would be ideal), several tubes of frosting gel, candies (like gumdrops, chocolate kisses and candy corn), animal crackers, or fancy cookies, and some coconut colored with food coloring. Everything would be set out on a table beforehand and it would be up to each girl to see what she could create.

And create they did. Midst munching, chattering, and giggling, Sarah's *Chocolate Cake* became a fortress with *Gingerman Cookies* manning peppermint stick rifles. Sally made a lovely castle with a *Vanilla Cake* with *Pirouette Cookies* holding up candy mint towers. Animal crackers in pretzel cages turned Kay's *Devil's Food Cake* into a circus wagon and Joan made an Easter scene with marshmallow chicks scattering jelly beans all over a *Coconut Cake*.

The birthday cake, which Karen did herself early in the day, was four *Golden Layer Cakes* placed side by side to form a large square. Using a wet knife, she smoothed the frosting over the seams making it look like one big cake. *Pirouette Cookies* with frosting dabbed on the top were lined up on the sides of the cake and they held the candles. On the top of the cake was a cut-out paper clown carrying a large flag that said Happy Birthday. And it was a happy birthday—or as Sarah put it, "...a real blast!"

LAYER CAKES

Place chocolate kisses around the top and bottom of a frozen *Vanilla Layer Cake*. Mix a sauce of half Amaretto and half orange juice; thicken with cornstarch mixed with water. Chill cake and sauce. Spoon sauce over each serving.

Mix canned, dark sweet cherries with Port wine and thicken with cornstarch. Chill. Serve *German Chocolate Layer Cake* cut into pieces with scoops of vanilla ice cream topped with cherry sauce.

Decorate a frozen *Coconut Layer Cake* with well-drained mandarin orange sections. Just before serving, sprinkle with crushed peanut brittle.

Whip heavy cream with sugar and vanilla. Fold in a little instant coffee. Spread mixture on a frozen *Chocolate Fudge Layer Cake*. Decorate top with well-drained maraschino cherries and pecan halves.

Frozen *Banana Cake Supreme* just before serving, can be topped with fresh banana slices and covered with whipped cream dusted with nutmeg.

Frozen *Boston Creme Cake Supreme* can be sprinkled with toasted sliced almonds or finely chopped candied orange peel or crystallized ginger.

Frozen *Chocolate Cake Supreme* can be placed on top of a block of coffee ice cream made by pressing ice cream into a foil-lined pan slightly larger than the cake. Freeze until hard, remove from pan using foil and place on serving platter. Top with cake and keep frozen until ready to serve. Cut into pieces down through the ice cream.

Sliver lemon rind and cook in clear corn syrup until translucent. Place on foil and separate. Sprinkle with sugar and let dry. Sprinkle around top edge of a frozen *Lemon Coconut Cake Supreme*.

Decorate a *Walnut Cake Supreme* with chocolate-covered peppermint patties cut into halves and placed cut-side down around top and bottom of cake.

OLD-FASHIONED CAKES

Purée canned, drained peaches or apricots and stir in a little Amaretto or orange liqueur and toasted slivered almonds. Spoon mixture over slices of *Pound Cake*.

Stir fruited or other flavored yogurt and spoon over slices of *Carrot Cake*. Sprinkle with toasted wheat germ.

Whip cream with sugar and a little cocoa or instant coffee. Fold in grated orange rind and mandarin orange sections. Spoon mixture over slices of *Carrot* or *Apple-Walnut Cake*.

Cook vanilla pudding (3-1/4-ounce package) using 3 cups of milk. Fold in rum flavoring and spoon while hot over slices of *Apple-Walnut Cake.*

Top *Pound Cake* with scoops of orange sherbet and spoonfuls of undrained, crushed pineapple.

Mash bananas and fold in chopped nuts and enough orange juice to make a sauce consistency. Spoon over *Apple-Walnut Cake* slices and sprinkle with toasted coconut.

Cut thin slices of *Pound Cake* and sandwich 2 slices of cake with slices of vanilla ice cream. Top with hot butterscotch sauce.

Layer cubes of *Carrot Cake* and vanilla yogurt in parfait glasses. Top with whipped cream and sprinkle with nutmeg.

Heat applesauce with a little brandy and a dash of cinnamon. Spoon while hot on slices of *Apple-Walnut Cake.*

Top *Pound Cake* slices with Peppermint ice cream and crushed peppermint candy.

Top *Pound Cake* slices with sugared fresh fruit or berries. Top with flavored yogurt or sour cream sprinkled with brown sugar.

Spread top and sides of *Date-Nut* cake with your favorite orange frosting. Sprinkle with chopped candied lemon peel.

Cut *Pound Cake* into 2 lengthwise layers and spread with apricot preserves. Spread top and sides with your favorite chocolate frosting.

GLAZES, TOPPINGS, AND SERVING SUGGESTIONS
FOR ANY OF THE FROZEN PIE TARTS, STRUDELS, OR TURNOVERS

Before baking, sprinkle or spread on
slivered almonds
flaked coconut
granulated sugar mixed with cinnamon
granulated sugar mixed with chopped nuts
apricot jam

After baking sprinkle with confectioners sugar while hot and again when cool.

After removing from oven, spread with a shiny glaze made by adding enough water to a cup of confectioners sugar to form a thin icing. Try with one of the many bottled ice cream toppings or crushed sweetened berries.

Excellent with whipped cream, a dollop of plain yogurt, or sour cream sweetened to taste.

Index

Acorn Squash, Stuffed, 39
Almond Chicken Snacks, 7
Almond Quiche, Haddock and, 68-70
Apple Cheese Logs, 122
Apricot-Almond Stuffing Mold, Chinese Chicken
    Wings With, 61-2
Apricot-Banana Refrigerator Cake, 142
Apricot Sausage Corn Bread, Chicken Stuffed
    With, 53
Apricot Stuffed Spareribs, 44-5
Apricot Swoons, 142
Artichoke and Hearts of Palm, Pickled, 93
Asparagus, Herbed, 102
Asparagus Newburg, Rock Lobster, 77-8
Avocado Orange Salad With Frozen Horseradish
    Cream, 112
Avocado Sandwich, Tuna, 124

Bacon Roll-Ups, Herb-Seasoned, 12
Baked Haddock, 67
Baklava, 143
Banana Bake, Sweet-Sour Turkey and, 49
Banana Coconut Bake, 141
Banana Grills, Wheat, 128
Banana-Pecan Herb Stuffing, Roast Turkey
    With, 58
Banana Refrigerator Cake, Apricot, 142
Banana Tarts, Chocolate, 143
Bass, Stuffed, 66
Bavarian Pot Roast, 37
Bean Salad, 108
Beans Meuniere, Yellow and Green, 104
Beef-and-Beer Stew, With Crouton Dumplings,
    Belgian, 32
Beef Pockets, Curried, 120
Beef Stuffed Mushrooms, 6
Beef Wellington, 37-8
Belgian Beef-and-Beer Stew With Crouton
    Dumplings, 32
Berry Crème Glacé in Patty Shells, 145
Berry Pie, Buttermilk, 145
Biscuits, quick ideas for, 151-2
Blue Cheese Mushroom Dip, 7
Blue Cheese Spread, 132
Bordeaux Cheese Torte, 135
Bouillon, Tomato, 19
Breads, quick ideas for, 147-8

Breads, quick sweet ideas for, 148
Broccoli and Cashew Nuts, Chinese
    Stir-Fried, 103-4
Broccoli and Egg Brunch, Creamed, 82
Broccoli au Gratin on Toasted Rolls, Halibut
    and, 71
Broccoli With Tuna Sauce, 97
Brown-and-serve breads and rolls, quick ideas
    for, 149
Brunch Scallop Kabobs, 65
Buttermilk Berry Pie, 145

Cabbage and Apples, Red, 94
Cabbage With Orange and Raisins, 100
Caesar Salad à la Pepperidge, 109
Candied Fruit Trifle, 138
Carrot and Nut Loaf, 101
Carrot Sticks, Crusty, 97
Casserole, Sunday Night, 94
Cauliflower Casserole, 100
Cauliflower Combo, 108
Celery Waldorf, 98
Cheese and Ham Loaf, Toasted, 122
Cheese and Pepper Sandwich Filling, Grilled, 130
Cheese Logs, Apple, 122
Cheese Sauce, Chicken in, 47
Cheese Soufflé, Easy, 84
Cheese Torte, Bordeaux, 135
Cheese Twists, 9
Cheese, Waffled Bread and, 89
Cheesey Potato Pancakes, 96
Cherry Jubilee Dessert, 134
Cherry Soup, Cold, 29-30
Chicken and Stuffing à la Waldorf, 47
Chicken Baskets, 129
Chicken Breasts, Sesame-Parsley Stuffed, 55
Chicken Divan, 62
Chicken in a Stuffing Nest, 52
Chicken in Cheese Sauce, 47
Chicken Liver Appetizer, 8
Chicken Livers Madeira, 51
Chicken Mold, Pineapple-Lime, 56
Chicken-on-the-Rye, 7
Chicken, Pan-Style Baked, 57
Chicken Snacks, Almond, 7
Chicken Stuffed With Apricot Sausage
    Corn Bread, 53

Chicken Triple Deckers, Cream Cheese &, 119
Chicken Vegetable Casserole, Herbed, 56
Chicken Wings With Apricot-Almond Stuffing, Mold, Chinese, 61-2
Chicken With Cream Gravy, Oven Fried, 60
Chiffon Pie, Walnut, 139
Chili Sloppy Joes, 126
Chili Stew With Cheese Pockets, Texas, 29
Chinese Cabbage, Lemon Veal and, 42
Chinese Chicken Wings With Apricot-Almond Stuffing Mold, 61-2
Chinese Cucumbers, Pickled, 9
Chinese Stir-Fried Broccoli and Cashew Nuts, 103-4
Chinese Stir-Fried Vegetables, 103
Chipped Beef and Pineapple Sandwich Filling, 130
Chocolate Banana Tarts, 143
Chocolate Delight, Yogurt-Peach, 136
Christmas Sandwich Wreath, 129-30
Cinnamon Raisin Crunch, 138
Cinnamon Soup, Hot, 23
Clam Stuffed Trout, 80
Coconut Bake, Banana, 141
Cod in a Crust, 64
Coquilles St. Jacques, 68
Corn Pudding, Irene's, 101
Corned Beef Spread, 16
Corny Seafood Bake, 72
Cottage Cheese Luncheon Salad, 116
Crab Deviled Egg, 17
Crab Soup, Curried, 21
Crab Stuffed Green Peppers, 70
Cream Cheese & Chicken Triple Deckers, 119
Cream Cheese Spread, 132
Cream Gravy, Oven Fried Chicken With, 60
Creamed Broccoli and Egg Brunch, 82
Crème Glacé in Patty Shells, Berry, 145
Croque Monsieur, Hot Deviled Ham, 121
Croutons, quick ideas for, 150
Crunchy Flounder Fillets, 74
Cucumber Spread, 10
Cucumber Yogurt Sandwich Filling, 130
Cucumbers, Pickled Chinese, 9
Curried Beef Pockets, 120
Curried Crab Soup, 21
Curried Shrimp, 79-80
Curried Tuna Spread, 15

Danish Prune Stuffed Duckling, 50
Deli Delight, 122-3
Desserts, Frozen, 152
Deviled Egg, Crab, 17
Deviled Seafood, 75
Dressings, 113, 115
Duckling, Danish Prune Stuffed, 50
Ducklings With Sumptuous Fruit Stuffing, 50
Dumplings, Stuffing, 19
Dutch Wilted Lettuce Salad, 107

Easy Cheese Soufflé, 86

Easy Haddock Mornay, 79
Egg and Green Pepper Sandwich Filling, 131
Egg Bake, Goldfish, 90
Egg Brunch, Creamed Broccoli and, 82
Egg Cups, Scrambled, 88
Egg Fu Yung, Shrimp, 87
Egg in a Crust, Russian Fish and, 78
Egg Scallop Scramble, 65
Eggplant Bake, Lamb and, 37
Eggplant Dip, 17
Eggplant Parmesan, 95
Eggplant Stew, French Lamb and, 28
Eggs Benedict, 85
Eggs Cordon Bleu, 89
Eggs Florentine, 88
Eggs in a Hole, 89
Eggs, Scotch, 90

Farmer Cheese and Pimiento-Olive Sandwich Filling, 130
Fish and Egg in a Crust, Russian, 78
Fish Chowder, New England, 31-2
Fish Stew, West Coast, 30-1
Flank Steak, Stuffed, 40
Flounder Fillets, Crunchy, 74
Fondue, Swiss, 83
Franks, Mini, 14
French Lamb and Eggplant Stew, 28
French Rolls Mediterranean Style, 120
French Toast Sandwiches, 91
Fruit Stuffing, Ducklings With Sumptuous, 50
Fruited Stuffed Goose, 53-5
Fruited Tuna Salad, 110
Fruits With Champagne, Pirouettes and, 135

Game Hens, Holiday, 59
Game Hens With Oyster Stuffing, 49
Garlic Crouton Frittata, 85
Gazpacho, 20
German Potatoes With Scallions and Celery, 102
Giblet Gravy, 57
Glazes, 156
Goldfish Egg Bake, 90
Goldfish Gala, 74
Goose, Fruited Stuffed, 53-4
Gravy, Giblet, 57
Greek Meat Pockets, 121
Green Beans Italienne, 104
Grilled Stuffed Spareribs, 34

Haddock and Almond Quiche, 68-70
Haddock, Baked, 67
Haddock Mornay, Easy, 79
Halibut and Broccoli au Gratin on Toasted Rolls, 71
Ham and Rye Casserole, 91
Ham Croque Monsieur, Hot Deviled, 121
Ham Divan, 34
Ham in a Blanket, Canned, 35
Ham Loaf, Toasted Cheese and, 122

Ham Turnovers, 42-3
Hamburger Pie, 35
Hangtown Fry in a Roll, 118
Hearts of Palm, Pickled Artichoke and, 93
Herb-Seasoned Bacon Roll-Ups, 12
Herbed Chicken Vegetable Casserole, 56
Holiday Game Hens, 59
Horseradish Cream, Avocado Orange Salad
    With, 112
Hungarian Pork and Vegetable Goulash, 28-9

Irish Stew, 24
Italian Meat Ball Sandwich, 125

Jamaica Pâté, 11

Kielbasi and Kraut Stew, 19
Kraut Stew, Kielbasi and, 19

Lamb and Eggplant Bake, 37
Lamb and Eggplant Stew, French, 28
Lamb, Mock Crown Roast of, 45
Lamburger Pies, Scotch, 39
Layer cakes, 155
Layer cakes, frozen, 153-4
Leftover cooked stuffing, ideas for, 150
Leftover dry stuffing mix, ideas for, 150-1
Lentil Soup Parmesan, 27
Liverwurst Pâté, 14
Lobster Asparagus Newburg, Rock, 77

Marinated Shrimp, 11
Meat and Potato Salad, Hot, 116
Meat Ball Sandwich, Italian, 125
Meat Loaf, Juicy, 40
Meat Pockets, Greek, 121
Melon Salad With Yogurt Dressing, Molded, 106
Mincemeat Cookie Dessert, 136
Mini Franks, 14
Mini Pizzas, 6
Mock Crown Roast of Lamb, 45
Muffins, quick ideas for, 150
Mushroom Dip, Blue Cheese, 7
Mushroom Rolls, Toasted, 12
Mushroom Stuffing Balls, 60
Mushroom Stuffing Cups, 59-60
Mushroom Stuffing Squares, 60
Mushroom Stuffing Sticks, 60
Mushrooms, Beef Stuffed, 6

Napoleons, Individual, 144
New England Fish Chowder, 31-2
Noodle Pudding, 87
Nut Loaf, Carrot and, 101

Old-fashioned cakes, 155-6
Onion Soup, Sprouted Wheat, 27
Orange and Raisins, Cabbage With, 100
Orange Cake, Frozen, 140
Orange Pico Salad, 113-4

Orange Pork Chops, Baked, 41
Orange Salad With Frozen Horseradish Cream,
    Avocado, 112
Orange Sweet Potato Pie, 96
Oven Fried Chicken With Cream Gravy, 60
Oyster Stew, 22
Oyster Stuffing, Game Hens With, 49

Pan-Style Baked Chicken, 57
Party Sandwich Loaf, 131-2
Pea Soup, Fresh, 30
Peach Melba Pirouette Cake, Frozen, 140
Peanut Soup, 22
Peas Epicurean, 93
Pepper-Filled Deli Rolls, Sausage and, 125-6
Pepper Sandwich Filling, Egg and Green, 131
Pepper Sandwich Filling, Grilled Cheese and, 130
Peppers, Crab Stuffed Green, 70
Peppers, Fruity Walnut Stuffed, 98
Perfection Salad, 114-5
Petite Pâté, 10
Pickled Chinese Cucumbers, 9
Pimiento-Olive Sandwich Filling, Farmer Cheese
    and, 130
Pineapple Fluff Pie, 139
Pineapple-Honey Wheatberry Bread Pudding, 141
Pineapple-Lime-Chicken Mold, 56
Pineapple Salad, 106
Pineapple Sandwich Filling, Chipped Beef and,
    130
Pineapple Soup, Chilled, 20
Piquant Sauce, 76
Pirouettes and Fruits With Champagne, 135
Pizza Pastries, 15
Pizzas, Mini, 6
Pork and Vegetable Goulash, Hungarian, 28-9
Pork Chops, Baked Orange, 41
Pork Chops in Foil, Stuffed, 41
Pork Roast, Easy, 44
Pot Roast, Bavarian, 37
Potato Pancakes, Cheesey, 96
Potato Salad, Hot Meat and, 116
Potatoes With Scallions and Celery, German,
    102
Potatoes With Sour Cream and Chive Topping,
    Scalloped, 95
Poultry, 46-62
Prune Stuffed Duckling, Danish, 50
Pumpernibbles, 14
Pumpernickel Sandwich, Open Face, 128-9
Pumpkin Bake, Creamy, 134

Quiche Lorraine, 83
Quick Dobos Torte, 144

Raisin Crunch, Cinnamon, 138
Raisins, Cabbage With Orange and, 100
Ratatouille Roll, Hot, 127
Red Snapper Diablo, 64
Rice Salad, Turkey, 109

Roast Turkey With Banana-Pecan Herb Stuffing, 58
Rolls, quick ideas for, 148-9
Rolls, quick sweet ideas for, 149
Russian Fish and Egg in a Crust, 78
Rye Bread Sauce, Salmon Stuffed Fillets With, 73

Salad Bar Buffet, 112-3
Salad Dressings, 113
Salade Niçoise, 107
Salmon Ball, 8
Salmon Mousse With Cucumber Dressing, 115
Salmon-Oatmeal Loaf, 76
Salmon Provençale, 72
Salmon Stuffed Fillets With Rye Bread Sauce, 73
Sandwich Fillings, 130-2
Sandwich pocket snack ideas, 149-50
Sandwich suggestions, 132
Sandwiches By The Inch, 119
Sandwiches, French Toast, 91
Sandwiches, Souffléed, 84
Sandwiches, Swedish, 16
Sausage and Pepper-Filled Deli Rolls, 125-6
Scallop Kabobs, Brunch, 65
Scallop Scramble, Egg, 65
Scotch Eggs, 90
Scotch Lamburger Pies, 39
Scrambled Egg Cups, 88
Seafood Bake, Corny, 72
Seafood, Deviled, 75
Seafood Newburg Vol-au-Vent, 76-7
Seafood Strata, 71
Sesame-Parsley Stuffed Chicken Breasts, 55
Shrimp Boats With Lemon Sails, 67
Shrimp, Curried, 79-80
Shrimp Egg Fu Yung, 87
Shrimp, Marinated, 11
Shrimps Mediterranean, 75
Sloppy Joes, Chili, 126
Soufflé, Easy Cheese, 84
Souffléed Sandwiches, 84
Sour Cream and Chive Topping, Scalloped Potatoes With, 95
Spareribs, Apricot Stuffed, 44-5
Spareribs, Grilled Stuffed, 38
Spinach Salad, 114
Spinach Soup, 23
Sprouted Wheat and Tuna Pie, 73
Sprouted Wheat Onion Soup, 27
Sprouted Wheat Party Loaf, 127-8
Stew, Irish, 26
Stews, 18-32
Stir-Fried Vegetables, Chinese, 103
Strawberry Soup, 25
Stuffed Bass, 66
Stuffing, 19, 47-51, 52-5, 57-60, 66, 70
Stuffing Dumplings, 19
Stuffing Orientale, Thighs With, 48

Stuffing Ring With Turkey à la King, 55
Sunday Brunch Puffs, 48
Super-Duper Sandwich, 118
Swedish Sandwiches, 16
Sweet Potato Herb Stuffing, Turkey Breast With, 51
Sweet Potato Pie, Orange, 96
Sweet-Sour Turkey and Banana Bake, 49
Swiss Fondue, 83

Taco Ensalada, 110
Texas Chili Stew With Cheese Pockets, 29
Thighs With Stuffing Orientale, 48
Three-Meat Stew With Dumplings, 25
Toasted Mushroom Rolls, 12
Tomato Bouillon, 19
Toppings, 156
Torte, Quick Dobos, 144
Trifle, Candied Fruit, 138
Trout, Clam Stuffed, 80
Tuna Avocado Sandwich, 124
Tuna Crunch Muffins, Hot, 126-7
Tuna Pie, Sprouted Wheat and, 73
Tuna Salad, Fruited, 110
Tuna Sauce, Broccoli With, 97
Tuna Spread, Curried, 11
Tuna Tetrazzini Goldfish Casserole, 66
Turkey à la King, Stuffing Ring With, 55
Turkey and Banana Bake, Sweet-Sour, 49
Turkey Breast With Sweet Potato Herb Stuffing, 51
Turkey Cantonese, 61
Turkey Rice Salad, 109
Turkey With Banana-Pecan Herb Stuffing, Roast, 58

Veal and Chinese Cabbage, Lemon, 42
Veal Oskar, 43
Vegetables, Herb Crusted, 101-2

Waffled Bread and Cheese, 89
Walnut Chiffon Pie, 139
Walnut Stuffed Peppers, Fruity, 98
Wedding Cake, 153
Welsh Rarebit, 82
West Coast Fish Stew, 30-1
Wheat Banana Grills, 128
Wheatberry Bread Pudding, Pineapple-Honey, 141
Wilted Lettuce Salad, Dutch, 107

Yogurt Dressing, Molded Melon Salad With, 106
Yogurt-Peach Chocolate Delight, 136
Yogurt Soup, Cold, 21

Zebra Loaf, 124
Zucchini Soup, 24